STAIRWAY
10 Steps to Heaven
Lars Gimstedt

© PsykosyntesForum, 2014

No part of this book may be reproduced in any form, except for the quotation of brief passages in criticism or reviews, without the expressed permission of the publisher: mail@psykosyntesforum.se.

Ideas expressed in this book are those of the author and do not reflect the views of The Foundation of Inner Peace, the publishers of *A Course in Miracles*.

Revision date June 22 2014.

ISBN
978-91-981738-0-2   (Kindle version)
978-91-981738-1-9   (EPUB version)
978-91-981738-2-6   (PDF version)
978-91-981738-3-3   (Paper back)

The Kindle version is available on Amazon.com and other Amazon internet stores. The other versions, including the Swedish versions, are available at http://psykosyntesforum.se/Stairway.htm

Book cover and illustrations designed by the author. Typefaces Bookman Old 12, Courier New 12 and Segoe Print 11. Page size 6x9" (15,24x22,86 cm) Margins: hor 2,0, vert 1,75.

About the author:

Lars Gimstedt works as a psychotherapist in Linkoping, Sweden. His formal training was as a quantum physicist, and he has worked as an engineer and a manager in corporate business for 30 years.

In the middle of his life, he started to study Psychosynthesis, CBT and NLP, and worked part time as a psychotherapist during ten years, until he started to work full time in his company PsychosynthesisForum.com in 2003 with life and leadership coaching, psychotherapy and with internet e-courses and e-books.

***

Stairway   Lars Gimstedt

"The book Stairway by Lars Gimstedt is an imaginative and thrilling vision about how mankind's development on Earth can be changed into something better. It is also a thoroughly documented description of how another book, A Course in Miracles (ACIM), can lead to a personal and spiritual growth against all odds.

Those who have worked with ACIM themselves will probably recognize things from their own experiences. But also for those that are beginners to ACIM, the book will convey ideas about how the Course influences, in ways that are both easy to understand and that are educating.

The book differs from an ordinary novel in its format. The different steps in Stairway are identified with the rainbow colors. The narrative consists of letters and reports in different formats and fonts, and it also includes images and symbols. The resulting variation makes the book beautiful, as well as more interesting and easier to read.

For myself, I found Lars' book very engaging and I recommend it for everyone that have worked with A Course in Miracles and for everyone wanting to learn more about the Course. His book reflects his deep knowledge and experience of ACIM in different situations and contexts. It describes an emerging vision where something deeper in us than the hunt for money and social status, and it is therefore a book for inspiration.

Albert Harloff, Stjarnsund, Sweden, April 27 2014."

(ACIM translator to Norwegian, author of Thy Will Be Done, chairman Swedish ACIM Network.)

Stairway   Lars Gimstedt

"Imagine a world dedicated to living the happy dream promised by 'A Course in Miracles'. All it would require is people experiencing the Holy Instant and living peacefully together.

Lars Gimstedt gives us a peek into the future. Fast forward 300 hundred years and the transformation is happening, but not without the group ego's last stand. For many people in future world, paranoia runs deep.

Read this book to find out what happens!"

(Dr. Sam Menahem, spiritual psychologist. Founder of the Center for Psychotherapy and Spiritual Growth.)

Stairway   Lars Gimstedt

Your stairway lies on the whispering wind

And as we wind on down the road

Our shadows taller than our soul

There walks a lady we all know

Who shines white light and wants to show

How everything still turns to gold

And if you listen very hard

The tune will come to you at last

When all are one and one is all

To be a rock and not to roll

(From the song "Stairway to Heaven"
by Jimmy Page & Robert Plant
on Led Zeppelin IV 1971)

Stairway Lars Gimstedt

Summary

John Zacharias, the typical engineer, became more and more provoked by his wife's growing interest in New Age, which he regarded as anti-scientific brainwashing.

When she one day asked him to read a pamphlet about a book that was alleged to have been "channeled" to the author from Jesus Christ, who had given it the title "A Course in Miracles", his patience hit a limit.

But, instead of trying again to persuade his wife into realizing why all this just was superstition and naïve wishful thinking, he strangely enough decided to read the book, in order to prove to her that it was all humbug.

This improbable decision changed John's life completely. Reading the book made John re-evaluate his view on reality, it made him change his profession into becoming a psychotherapist, and it ultimately made him learn to listen to the divine inner guidance that exists in the silent bottom of the mind of everyone.

John's inner guidance led him onto a life-long path towards enlightenment. On his way there, he discovered and refined the ability to transport himself through space and time.

This ability was registered by the global security system TSS that by 2040 had become refined to a level of sophistication where it could maintain constant surveillance of every individual on Earth.

When John, after having disappeared without a trace on his hundredth birthday in 2046, returned after three hundred years, many authorities saw John's return as a grave security risk that eventually could jeopardize political control. The space-time jump ability had from 2144 slowly spread to others. Fearing a more rapid increase of this ability due to John's return, a special office within the NSA was now formed and was assigned the task of investigating, containing and eliminating this risk.

But, darkness can never dispel Light. The book Stairway is about John's spiritual path to enlightenment, and about what will happen to mankind when more and more of us let our Inner Light shine, and how this ultimately will dispel all darkness.

Index

Summary 7

October 19, 2346. NSA Report. 11

December 19, 2346.
BLOG ENTRY: Seeks – Context. 17

December 28, 2346. NSA Report. 33

January 2, 2347. Stairway New Zealand News. 37

January 19, 2347.
BLOG ENTRY: Finding Traces – Action. 44

January 23, 2347. NSA Report. 55

January 30, 2347. Stairway New Zealand News. 58

March 23, 2347.
BLOG ENTRY: Finding the Bull – Skill. 61

March 27, 2347. NSA Report. 76

March 30, 2347. Stairway New Zealand News. 78

May 18, 2347.
BLOG ENTRY: Catching the Bull – Reality. 83

May 22, 2347. NSA Report. 100

May 30, 2347. Stairway New Zealand News. 103

July 20, 2347.
BLOG ENTRY: Gentling the Bull – Beliefs. 107

July 24, 2347. NSA Report. 120

July 30, 2347. Stairway New Zealand News. 123

September 19, 2347.
BLOG ENTRY: Returning Home – Values. 131

September 23, 2347. NSA Report. 145

September 30, 2347. Stairway New Zealand News. 148

November 16, 2347.
BLOG ENTRY: Bull Forgotten – Self-image. 154

November 20, 2347. NSA Report. 167

November 30, 2347. Stairway New Zealand News. 171

January 18, 2348.
BLOG ENTRY: Man Forgotten – The Mission. 176

January 22, 2348. NSA Report. 187

January 30, 2348. Stairway New Zealand News. 190

March 21, 2348.
BLOG ENTRY: The Origin – The Vision. 194

March 25, 2348. NSA Report. 210

March 30, 2348. Stairway New Zealand News. 213

June 11, 2348. NSA Report. 221

June 30, 2348. Stairway New Zealand News. 224

July 2, 2348. NSA Report. 228

July 30, 2348. Stairway New Zealand News. 230

October 15, 2348. NSA Report. 234

October 30, 2348. Stairway New Zealand News. 236

December 25, 2348.
BLOG ENTRY: Bestowing Bliss – Oneness. 240

December 30, 2348. Stairway New Zealand News. 259

January 9, 2349. NSA Report. 263

Appendix A: Key events 266

October 19, 2346. NSA Report.

****

NSA Report 2346-1001-3632
TOP SECRET. CLF code 0.
Department for The Transhuman Threat.
October 19 2346.
Unmonitored disappearances.
Case study TTT-JZ-1.

****

This report has been compiled in order to serve as background material in NSA-TTT's and others' ongoing investigations in unmonitored disappearances, which have been assessed as a mayor security risk to NATO, an assessment shared by other security agencies (see Attachment 1).

The security risk is coupled to hitherto unexplained disappearances of individuals, in many cases despite these having been under strict physical observation or with close proximity probe surveillance. Many of these have after a while been detected again, but the re-appearances in themselves have up to now not been possible to document. All surveillance probes, now more than 2.300.000 units, placed in all countries, have been updated with new detection algorithms designed to trigger on connection glitches or terminations.

Stairway Lars Gimstedt

The first re-appearance that has been positively detected and documented by NSA has now occurred: September 19 2346, exactly 300 years after his disappearance, the rematerialization of Mr. John Zacharias has been detected at a distance from his old home on Iceland, located inside the Reykjavik Stairway Center on the small island Videy northwest of Reykjavik. John Zacharias seems to have a biological age of 100 years, the same age he had when he disappeared September 19 2046.

The disappearances have not been possible to couple to terrorism or other hostile actions towards NATO, nations or groups, but this risk must be taken into account. The prime reason for this is that the disappearances and the re-appearances severely disturb TSS, The Total Surveillance System, when the data acquisition from the surveillance probes located all over the world becomes terminated, and automatic re-connection is not triggered at the re-appearances, resulting in the existence of non-surveilled individuals, a grave security risk by itself. For example, in subsequent disappearances and re-appearances of Mr. Zacharias, it has taken TSS several days to start tracking Mr. Zacharias.

Of security reasons, this report does not disclose the identities of the persons and/or task force responsible to compiling this report, or future reports from NSA-TTT.

Stairway Lars Gimstedt

The disappearances seem in many cases have had connections with the so called Stairway movement, a loosely connected network, started in 2015 by the mentioned John Zacharias, at that time living in Seattle, USA. This network communicates in a seemingly unorganized way around spiritual development via a strict method for mind training as defined in a more than 360 years old book, "A Course in Miracles" (abbreviated ACIM from here on). The Stairway movement originally started out of an internet course, "A Psychosynthesis Perspective on ACIM", which Mr. Zacharias had compiled 2013 on the base of his twenty years' experience of applying the mind training methods of ACIM in his psychotherapeutic practice. Over a period of eight years the different study groups of the course slowly formed a network that eventually grew into an organization. It took its name 2022 after the title of a book John Zacharias wrote 2021, "Stairway to Heaven".

Mr. Zacharias' disappearance in 2046 was the first TSS documented loss of tracking case, where neither his dead body or Mr. Zacharias himself alive could be traced.

The first case of disappearance of this kind, where documentation still exists, although the scientific value of this narrative has been disputed, is the disappearance of the body of Jesus, as reported in The Bible. The reason for mentioning this is that Jesus is the alleged author of ACIM.

ACIM was first published 1976, and was by the publisher claimed to be the result of "channeling" from Jesus to a psychology professor Helen Schucman. Later disappearance and re-appearance of John Zacharias at a date long after a normal human lifespan gives reasons to believe that Jesus could in fact have been present during the years 1965 to 1972, and that the material could have been transferred by Brainwave Quantum Resonance Field (BQRF). Other cases of information transfer via BQRF have been scientifically investigated and documented as early as 2210 (Attachment 2).

Case Study TTT-JZ-1, which this document is the first report from, was initiated by the reappearance of John Zacharias. (He will be referred to with the abbreviation JZ from here.)

This reappearance is the first TSS has documented by probe activation, although there has been non-probe documentation from other sources about other disappearances and subsequent reappearances by JZ in the period from 2040 to 2046, and similar disappearances and re-appearances by other individuals during the period from year 2144 and forward. In order to gather scientific data for building up an understanding of the disappearance mechanisms, JZ will now be subjected to the highest level of probe monitoring, and NSA will continuously report the findings.

JZ worked as an engineer at Boeing, Seattle, for thirty years. Boeing at that time developed and produced airfoil vehicles, called aeroplanes (the Gravity Drive had not yet been invented). Via the so called New-Age movement, that had its main activities on the American west coast during the last decades of the twentieth century, JZ came into contact with ACIM in 1985. The impact of reading the book and of practicing the psychological training in ACIM made JZ to change his career from development engineer and manager to becoming a psychotherapist 1992, within the psychological school of Psychosynthesis.

Psychosynthesis was one of the first psychologies during the beginning of the twentieth century to describe what it called a "transpersonal realm" of reality, which seems to be a similar description as offered by ACIM. This "transpersonal realm" seems to constitute one possible explanation of the disappearances, but this has not been possible to confirm with any known scientific methods.

We think it may be important to make oneself acquainted with the mind training techniques of ACIM's, and with the thought system and the life history of JZ, because this knowledge is deemed as crucial in the continued investigation of the unexplained phenomena of disappearances and re-appearances, or with a more stringent term, re-materializations .

Coming investigations will focus on publications by and about JZ not as yet analyzed by NSA, and will naturally also focus heavily on the future activities of JZ.

So far the probe monitoring and remote monitoring of JZ has worked well, although with unexplained glitches in the contact. Automatic re-establishing of the tracking has up to now also worked well, but JZ has at each of these cases changed location, sometimes to places very far from where the TSS tracking was interrupted.

****

End of NSA Report 2346-1001-3632
TOP SECRET. CLF code 0.
October 19 2346.

****

Stairway Lars Gimstedt

December 19, 2346.
BLOG ENTRY: Seeks – Context.

1. Seeks.   **Context.**

Welcome to my blog

Thank you, dear reader, for visiting my new blog!

I assume that the reason you have found this blog is that someone told you it was here, giving you the web address, or that you as a Stairway member has received information from your local center.

I also assume that, whatever other reasons you may have to have come here, one is surely curiosity: how can a person that vanished 300 years ago be here again, and how is it possible for John Zacharias to be 400 years old?

I can assure you that I am only one hundred years old, and in good health. I have returned for a number of reasons, which I will tell you more about in coming blog entries. One of the reasons is to write this blog, in which I will begin to describe my life before 2046. I want to do this in order to correct some of the misunderstandings and myths about me that have evolved during the last three hundred years. I also want to do this to help the ones of you reading my blog to follow the path of spiritual awakening I, and others before me, have taken.

Stairway   Lars Gimstedt

In order to let what I tell you to sink in, and in order to give you time to discuss it with each other, I will make entries in this blog only now and then. So click on the 'follow' button above the header if you wish to be notified about blog updates.

Of technical and security reasons, you cannot leave comments underneath, but you are welcome to mail me at my old e-mail mail@psykosyntesforum.se , which is coupled to my old website psychosynthesisforum.com, that the main Stairway Center has kept active all these years.

I live in my old home on Videy, Iceland, which the Stairway Center of Iceland has kept in good order. I was really amazed when I saw all the things that had happened here at the Main Center since I left 2046, with all the new buildings.

I have been contacted by the TSS people, of course, but all in all they have remained passive, even if I suspect that there are numerous specialized probes watching each step I take…

The header image

I have put an image in the header of this blog. This image is a part of a larger one, which will gradually appear, more in each coming blog entry. The image will denote which step on my path to awakening I will write about. The definition of the steps is based on an old Buddhist tradition, ten meditation focus pictures called The Bull and His Herdsman. These pictures, together with koans (short poems) were used from the 12th century for mind training. Look at one version that I have set up a long time ago at http://psykosyntesforum.se/PsF_0892_The_Bull/PsF_0892_The_Bull_1.html, where you even can listen to me reading the description texts underneath the pictures and the three koans that poetically comment each picture.

On the right side of the header image, I have also made a connection between this Buddhist tradition and the mind training format from Gregory Bateson's cybernetic theory of Logical Levels, from 1951. Logical Levels was later used by Richard Bandler and John Grinder in the development of Neurolinguistic Programming, NLP, a psychology I often used in my practice as a psychotherapist, together with Psychosynthesis.

But now, to my story of my own journey, a journey of personal and spiritual development and awakening.

The first turning point

When I turned forty, in September 1986, I had for my whole life had the engineer's secure and logical view of the world: reality was controlled by the laws of nature. Even if much was still unclear at that time - quantum physicists had just started to report strange things around cause and effect - the laws of nature made me feel comfortable. Much was still unknown, but it would only be a matter of time - the knowledge about the world had increased for each generation during many hundreds of years, and would continue to increase, in an accelerated rate.

The religious persons could occupy themselves with whatever they were doing, I did not care. I saw myself as a friendly and tolerant person (which I still do).
I realized that people were different, and it was understandable and of little real importance to me that some had not come as far in their knowledge as others, making it necessary for them to use metaphysical explanations instead of physical.
I trusted that the increasing knowledge from science would make more and more people to let go of their old superstitions. I was forty years old, and I had a long formal training as a quantum physicist and fifteen years professional experience as an aerospace engineer as my intellectual foundation.

What I could not understand was when people criticized science for being inhuman and ugly. For myself, I could feel uplifted when I saw the results of a computer program I had developed, making a simulator work like a real airplane. I could even get a strong experience of the inherent beauty of fine technology, when the control laws I had developed in the simulator made the test pilot talk about the airplane as if he was a horseman talking about a beautiful horse.

I felt open-minded and tolerant towards about others, and I felt the same way towards my wife Anna as well, despite her interest in para-psychology and other New Age stuff (New Age was the umbrella term for a movement around spiritual awakening that started on the American west coast in the 1970's). I sometimes discussed these things with her, when she had read some article or book, but I never succeeded in convincing her of my own firm belief: everything she talked about had or would ultimately get a scientific explanation, even if more research might be needed to understand the underlying mechanisms, research that might require years or even decades. But I did not try to push her – I was sure she would accept this undisputable fact over time.

But when Anna started to attend meetings with mediums and fortune-tellers, I got more disturbed. The more she enthusiastically talked about the "fantastic" things she had heard about, the more irritated I felt, and I also felt frustrated by her naïveté.

Anna's interest in New Age increased more and more during a couple of years, and she often talked about how the things she had heard about would bring mankind into a new era, the "New Age". My patience was wearing thin, and this made our discussions more and more strained, until she finally did not want to discuss these things with me anymore, accusing me for being narrow-minded and dull.

Anna's social life began include more and more New Age people, and when we had guests, or we were visiting others, I began to feel increasingly excluded. It even felt like they looked down on me when I kept myself outside their discussions.

This had a negative impact on mine and Anna's relationship, and I felt more and more frustrated. I brooded a lot about whether we could find the way back to each other again, and I longed back to the time when we still could discuss our different views on reality, as adult and mature people.

But one day in the fall of 1986 something happened, which I much later in my life would regard as the first real turning-point onto the path of inner transformation I was going to travel. Anna came home with a pamphlet she had got when attending a seminar at the New Age café downtown Seattle that she frequented. She wanted to tell me about the seminar, but asked me to read the pamphlet first, so that I would at least have the full information "before coming with all my usual objections" as she expressed it.

The pamphlet was about a New Age book that had come into existence through "channeling". A woman had heard "an inner dictation" from a person who later had identified himself as Jesus. This inner dictation continued every day during a period of seven years, and after a while it resulted in the publication of a book called "A Course in Miracles", further on in the pamphlet abbreviated as ACIM. The book was subdivided into three parts: one textbook with theory, one workbook with 365 lessons, and a manual for teachers.

(I assume that most of you reading this blog are well acquainted with ACIM, but I will continue to include full information like this for the benefit of those of you who are new to the Stairway Movement.)

I obediently read the pamphlet, but I felt more irritation and frustration than ever before – this was worse and crazier than anything else she had come home with over the years. The pamphlet not only talked about the Transpersonal or Spiritual realm of reality, it claimed that the physical reality was an illusion all together! I started to wonder whether Anna was becoming the victim of some occult sect, and I felt genuine anxiety and helplessness.

At that exact moment the thing happened, which I later would come to regard as a turning-point for me: the thought came up in my mind that I had to "save" Anna, by making a decision I later could feel amazed I even would consider: I decided to buy the book and to read it from cover to cover, in order to be able to prove to Anna once and for all that meta-physical hosh-posh will ultimately lead to losing one's grip of reality. I made this decision despite the fact that the pamphlet described the book as heavy reading and as very extensive - more than 1200 pages long.

I bought the book at the café, and set aside an hour each evening to read it, after I had come home from my work, we had had dinner and had put our two children, four and seven at the time, to bed.

Already in the introduction, A Course in Miracles described how it came to be: how the psychology professor Helen Schucman, after having had inner strange visions during a large number of years, thought that she had gone crazy when an "inner dictation" started. How she confided in her boss on the psychology institution of Columbia University, and how he offered to help her to make notes of what she had heard, before deciding what to do about it.

Stairway Lars Gimstedt

I felt very disturbed about how two scientifically highly trained persons could have ended up in this kind of muddled thought patterns, and I more and more believed that Helen Schucman had become the victim of some kind of psychological disorder, and that her boss Bill Thetford had become psychologically co-dependent in what in psychological literature is called a "folie à deux".

But, a mere suspicion like this could be easily dismissed by Anna as just having my usual negative and judgmental attitude, and as I had taken on the task of proving the falsehood of ACIM, I persevered in my reading. The book really was heavy reading – each sentence felt charged with meaning and hidden clues. That the text was formed in Shakespeare's meter Iambic Pentameter did not make my task any easier.

As I all the time had my focus on finding traces of psychological disorder and confusion in what I read, I after some days of reading became increasingly confused about the total lack of this. Everything I read felt logical, well thought through and very structured. I noticed that the text often referred to other parts both earlier and later in the book, in a way that conveyed that the person having compiled this text was in total control of the entirety of the subject.

I began reluctantly to take in what the book actually said, and my focus on Helen Schucman, Bill Thetford, and their "folie à deux" abated more and more. Instead, I now started to become disturbed over something else than the story of how ACIM came into existence: I found that what I read awoke something inside of me. I felt sympathy to the part of the message that was about acceptance and forgiveness, as this matched my own core values. But even the part of the message that on an intellectual level felt completely alien, that the physical world is a mental projection made up by a collective mind, created some kind of resonance deep inside myself, even though my conscious and scientific mind revolted to the thought.

It took me a couple of months to read the textbook part, a little more than 600 pages. I had originally thought that I would read extensively, scanning through the material to look after "proof of insanity", but I found myself reading slower and slower, to allow each word, each sentence, each concept, to sink in.

When I came to the second part of the book, the 365 lessons, I decided to actually "take" the course - I read and meditated on one lesson each day. I started each day by reading the lesson, memorizing the instructions about how it was to be done during the day. I even bought a cheap digital watch that I could make sound a short beep on the hour, reminding me to repeat the lesson regularly during the day, according to the instructions given.

One could now have thought, that this change of my attitude would have improved my and Anna's relationship, as I now had started to come over "on her side". But, for Anna the pamphlet about "A Course in Miracles" had been not much more than another interesting example of fascinating New Age phenomena. At the start of my reading she enjoyed discussing it with me, but after a while my total focus on the task I had taken on made her lose interest in our discussions, and we grew apart again. And my original goal, of "saving" her from delusion, had obviously been replaced by something I could not even clarify to myself.

I began to ruminate a lot about my old notion of reality, trying to figure out how science and ACIMs metaphysics could possibly co-exist. I was never prepared to abandon science, but I started to open up to the notion that science is maybe not able to describe *all* of reality, even if it is able to describe everything physically observable and measurable. But still, the first lessons of ACIM continued to disturb my old scientific sense of secure stability:

> *Lesson 1. Nothing I see means anything.*
>
> *Lesson 2. I have given everything I see all the meaning that it has for me.*
>
> *Lesson 3. I do not understand anything I see.*
>
> *Lesson 4. These thoughts do not mean anything.*
>
> *Lesson 5. I am never upset for the reason I think.*

My ruminations and my constant brooding soon led to an emotional and existential crisis, and I started to isolate myself from others. I became a full-fledged spiritual seeker, and searched through numerous New Age book stores for other books that maybe could help me to understand. My sense of reality

Stairway

began to feel swampy and fuzzy, and I looked for alternate descriptions in books about Buddhism, meditation, Zen, Christian and Islamic mysticism.

I found many other publications, where the author claimed to have received the content from Jesus. These were seldom as extensive as ACIM, but I became severely disturbed by how they often contradicted each other and contradicted ACIM, even if much of the concepts often were the same.

I attended a seminar on ACIM held in Seattle, were the main point on the agenda was a presentation by Kenneth Wapnick, the person who had edited ACIM after the original manuscript had been finalized. Many posed questions to Kenneth, but I wanted to be alone with him, so I waited until the meeting had ended and everyone else had left. When I finally could get Kenneth to myself, I told him about my spiritual journey that had just started, about my confusion and anxiety, and my frustration about all the other different channeled messages from Jesus. Kenneth listened patiently until I had finished describing my problems, then with a friendly laugh, he put his hand on my shoulder and said *"If we would confront everyone claiming to talk with the voice of Jesus, we would not have the time to do anything else. Continue your study of the Course, and make up your own mind. Good luck!"* And with this he excused himself, saying he had a flight to catch and we parted. I felt a little put off, but at the same time felt relieved - Kenneth did not seem like a sect-leader or guru or anything near this.

Stairway   Lars Gimstedt

I continued my search, and decided to try to find some kind of community, where ACIM was discussed. In the suburb of Seattle where I lived with my family there was none within practical distance, and I decided to form my own community by arranging an evening course on ACIM, out of my belief that a good way of learning something is to teach it.

Putting together the material and leading this evening course forced me to formulate the message of ACIM in my own words, and I compiled a course material much based on pictures and diagrams, which suited my engineer side well. Being a course leader for a quite heterogeneous group of people was a useful experience for me, having had worked with computers, machines and engineers all my life.

During the period of leading the evening course, I went through the whole textbook once again, and I started to make the lessons a second time. Now I had bought all the lessons printed on small cards, so that I could bring the lesson of the day with me all day.

As the lessons are based on psychological methods as meditation, affirmation, visualization and similar, I also started to take a larger interest in psychology, and to my spiritual search I now added many popular-science books in psychology.

As Anna also had an interest in psychology, we started to have interesting discussions again, and after a while it felt like we were coming closer again. But, my intense, not to say fanatical, thirst for knowledge and spiritual insights made us grow apart again, as Anna never could relate to or understand the extent of my spiritual crisis. And for my part, I was so intensely focused on the purely intellectual aspect my spiritual search that I forgot to communicate in an authentic way. Monologue may be OK for a course leader, but works poorly in a marriage.

I learned much later in my life that *relating* to another person in an authentic way comes out of *communicating* in an authentic and honest way. As I functioned now, our relationship became reduced to every-day chores, parenthood and "managing" the "project" The Family.

The second turning point

As a part of my search, and due to my newly awakened interest in psychology, I signed up for a week-long course in Psychosynthesis, as the information material about the course described it as a kind of psychology that included the spiritual realm and that regarded the essence of a human being as spiritual.

The course, "Essentials of Psychosynthesis", was a totally new experience for me, as it was based on experiential learning, with many non-verbal exercises like guided imagery, role play, and free drawing. In the course, I became aware of strong similarities between the Psychosynthesis description of what it is to be a human being, and ACIM's description of our inner nature.

What I much later would regard as "the second turning point" came after having attended just four days of the course: I decided to sign up for a four year formal training to become a Psychosynthesis Therapist. I felt strongly that Psychosynthesis could constitute a practical and concrete path to manifesting the message of ACIM in my life, but I could not explain to others or to myself why I believed this.

Anna became surprised, naturally, but supported my decision, despite the economic burden I now had added to our family. My elderly parents on the other hand, that had looked forward to see me continue my career in corporate business, became worried: *"John has been snared by a religious sect"*.

The Psychosynthesis training made me launch on an "inner journey" towards learning to know myself, and towards learning to become aware of my Inner Higher Spiritual I, which Psychosynthesis calls the Self with capital S. The training also constituted, in the same way as the evening course I had led a couple of years earlier, but much more, a thorough learning of group psychology. Learning to adjust to twenty others with different personalities, in close co-operation during four years. Learning conflict resolution and learning to develop one's ability for empathy.

As revolutionary ACIM had been for how one can regard reality and the physical world, as revolutionary was the Psychosynthesis training for how one can regard oneself, and for getting to know who one really is, beneath one's façade and role-playing.

Stairway Lars Gimstedt

Lost in the dust

These two intense, and long, inner journeys of mine that had taken up all my time and energy, had now brought Anna and me so far apart, that Anna entered a relationship with another man, and this led to a divorce, painful for us both. It coincided with an unusually rainy and cold fall in 1991.

And everything fell apart for me, who had always regarded myself as a family man, a good father and a loving and loyal partner. But thanks to the firm support from my course leaders, from my personal therapist (participants in the Psychosynthesis training had to get personal therapy) and from my friends in the training, I managed to come through the painful process of divorce and of separation from my children, even if I still had weekend contact with them. They were 11 and 13 at the time.

It felt as trying to awaken, to wanting to find something bigger than my previous reality, had only led to suffocating pain and suffering. Instead of knowing more, it now felt like I knew less than ever, five years after "the first turning point", and I did not have a clue of where in life I was.

The header for this blog entry is Search – Context. The first image in The Bull and His Herdsman and the text below reminded me of how I had decided to search for something of crucial importance for me, but how I now had come completely astray:

Stairway   Lars Gimstedt

The search for what? The bull has never been missing.

But without knowing it the herdsman estranged himself from himself and so the bull became lost in the dust.

The home mountains recede ever further, and suddenly the herdsman finds himself on entangled paths.

Lust for gain and fear of loss flare up like a conflagration, and views of right and wrong oppose each other like spears on a battlefield.

But, at the same time, looking at how the Herdsman's journey continued in the book, this text still felt somehow comforting. Others had obviously had the same experience as I, and survived...

Stairway Lars Gimstedt

December 28, 2346. NSA Report.

****

NSA Report 2346-1001-3715
TOP SECRET. CLF code 0.
Department for The Transhuman Threat.
December 28 2346.
Unmonitored disappearances.
Case study TTT-JZ-1.

****

The Case study JZ-1 has with the appearance December 19 of a new internet blog by JZ been accelerated, with an increased number of investigators, and with enhanced probe monitoring. To optimize security, the decision has been made at NSA, to limit JZ's contacts with others as much as possible, within the local national laws. As he has not violated any law, we cannot at present isolate him physically.

To the unknown mechanisms behind JZ's disappearances and re-appearances has now come another disturbing factor: the blog has proven impossible to trace to any specific server, making it impossible to close down. Analysis of the IP transfer codes has shown that it uses a hitherto unknown cryptography method, by which the IP data packets travel in unconventional ways through the web, and it also self-erases sender data at any attempt to read or divert the data stream. This constitutes a new security risk that by itself has initiated a new NSA-TTT task force.

This report attempts to analyze JZ's motives and plans.

One of JZ's motives seems to be to activate others to learn the method for BQRF invisibility impact, the hypothesis NSA-TTT holds at present for the disappearances. This is described below.

We have no information about JZ's plans except for one part of his plan, which is to return with new blog entries, although the time schedule for this is not revealed.

In addition to publishing himself on the internet, he has "travelled" some, by disappearances and then re-appearing, always at a Stairway Center somewhere. To date he has visited four of these, staying a couple of days each time. The rest of his time he seems to spend in inactivity in his home on Iceland.

In his blog JZ describes his way from being an ordinary and unknown person, an engineer and a non-reflecting atheist, to becoming a promoter of ACIM ("A Course in Miracles", see the previous report, 2346-1001-3632,) in his book "The Stairway to Heaven". As we all know, his book and JZ himself became a worldwide celebrity after his first disappearance, and subsequent periods of non-traceability during the period 2040 to 2046. At the end of this period he disappeared the day he turned one hundred years, and as reported in our previous report he now has re-appeared after exactly 300 years. The short periods of non-traceability have continued after this, combined with unmonitored movements over long distances.

The relevance of JZ's blog entry is mainly the description of the impact of the combination of the mind training methods as taught by ACIM, and the psychological models and methods of Psychosynthesis.

One theory, which should be affirmed through experimental verification on subjects with similar personality typology, is that a combined ACIM/Psychosynthesis mind training could maybe lead to an enhanced mind control of BQRF (Brainwave Quantum Resonance Field), by which trained subjects can alter the perception of others, so that the subject turns invisible. This mechanism could also include hypnotic factors, which might be why JZ studied NLP, which utilizes hypnosis techniques of different kinds.

So, the main relevance here is to understand the drastic changes in basic personality and thought patterns that this stage of JZ's life led to, and to correlate these changes to other individuals involved in cases of unexplained disappearances.

****

End of NSA Report 2346-1001-3715
TOP SECRET. CLF code 0.
December 28 2346.

****

Stairway   Lars Gimstedt

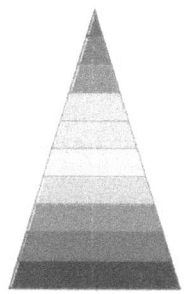

January 2, 2347.
Stairway New Zealand News.

Dear Sisters and Brothers

A very long time ago, we at Stairway New Zealand issued membership newsletters. The last one was two hundred years ago, September 2150. Due to a lot of repressive activities of the NSA, the Center then decided to close down the newsletter distributed by com messages (at that time called e-mails), and instead issued information verbally at our monthly meetings here in Auckland.

Now, after the fantastic return of John Zacharias, we have decided to again issue newsletters. To protect your integrity, it will be written by hand and photocopied, like this one is, and distributed by hand by a number of us here at the Center.

Stairway   Lars Gimstedt

I, with the pencil now in my hand, am Lena Adamson, who most of you probably have met at our meetings. I am Information Manager here at our Center, a position I have had for five years now.

To my knowledge, this is the first time information has been spread in this way, with this method, since the twentieth century!

The initiative for re-starting the newsletter was the unanimous decision we took at our large member meeting in Auckland September 25, when we had heard about John's return September 19:th. I guess most of you reading this were there.

I assume that you have heard of and have read John's blog, so I will in these newsletters not repeat things he already has given information on. We have taken up this newsletter in order to better answer all questions different persons here at Stairway New Zealand get from our members. We want to ensure that you all will be getting the same information from us.

It has taken us until now to get hold of photocopy equipment, which wasn't easy - we managed to assemble it from old museum parts.

Stairway Lars Gimstedt

But we are happy to be able to release the first issue now, just after John's first blog entry.

Despite knowing a lot about John from everything that has been written about him during the last 300 years, and despite almost knowing "Stairway to Heaven" by heart, I for one am looking forward to read the continuation of John's own version of his path to Awakening. And I think many of you share my anticipation. I think, and I hope, that his story will be useful in our own individual inner journeys.

But, I can't really speculate on what you, dear Sisters and Brothers, will get from John's blog, so in these newsletters I will just try to write about my <u>own</u> personal thoughts and reactions, and I will try to give <u>my</u> personal answers and clarifications on the questions we get.

After all, with only ten years' studies of ACIM behind me, I am still a novice compared to many of you, and certainly compared to John, who has sixty years' experience, maybe even three hundred sixty…

Now, to John's blog.

"The Bull"

Even if John used the meditation images from "The Bull and His Herdsman" already in his first web course about ACIM in 2013, and used them a bit more in his book, this is the first time he uses "The Bull Images" as a structure for his description of his own spiritual path. It seems like Buddhism has been more important for John than I knew. But, I am rather sure that the importance of Buddhism for John is equal to the importance of any religious schools – he uses the religious language as tools to convey his message. Just as ACIM uses the Christian language, often in ways that Christian literal believers still have difficulties accepting.

As ACIM says in the Manual, "Who are God's teachers?":

> "A teacher of God is anyone who chooses to be one."

> "They come from all over the world.
> They come from all religions and from no religion."

> "There is a course for every teacher of God. The form of the course varies greatly. So do the

particular teaching aids involved. But the content of the course never changes."

"Lost in the dust"

Reading John's story about his initial awakening, and how he almost reverted to fanaticism for a while, was sobering for me, as I have always regarded John as some kind of mythical saint. He comes out to be as a rather ordinary human being, and I can really relate to his difficulties, even if my own path has been different.

In the beginning of my own studies of ACIM ten years ago, I had none I could talk to about my thoughts, and I felt completely alone. I was much younger than John was when he came across ACIM, I was only 20. For me, reading ACIM didn't make me change my profession or anything like that, but it really made all my previous "life plans" feel obsolete. And like John, I also had a very long period of feeling "lost in the dust".

When reading about what he calls his "turning points", I could recall a couple of inexplicable things that happened to me that I really now can see as turning points on my own spiritual path, and that eventually led to me

Stairway — Lars Gimstedt

becoming employed here at the Center as Information Manager.

In my contacts with you members over the five years I have been working here at the Stairway Center, I have heard many talk about similar seemingly random things that happened to them, that long afterwards have felt like they have not been chance happenings at all – on the contrary many have felt that these "synchronistic" events were the result of divine intervention.

For me the question whether God Himself has intervened, or if it is my own Higher I – my Self – that has "pushed me in the right direction" is not really important for me. Personally, I am convinced that _if_ I really can distinguish between my Self and my ego, then I can trust my intuition. <u>Then</u> the "voice" I hear _is_ from God, even if it has travelled through The Holy Spirit, or my Self, and in the process gone from the formless to a certain form I can understand and accept.

I think this is one of ACIM's purposes, learning us to be able to make this distinction, knowing whose inner voice we are hearing, the ego's or the Self's.

Stairway Lars Gimstedt

Until next time, with love

Lena Adamson

January 19, 2347.
BLOG ENTRY: Finding Traces – Action.

Welcome back to the blog of John Zacharias.

I first of all want to thank the Centers I have visited, for their hospitality, loving kindness, and for our fruitful discussions.
I am looking forward to meeting with you all in the other Centers, but my plan for this is still not established.

The TSS people have been here a lot, going through our files and our computers, but they have found nothing not complying with NSA rules. Most of them behave in in a courteous but a bit formal manner, but with some of them we have had quite interesting discussions.

In the last entry I wrote about the start of my spiritual awakening, about two turning points (I of course know today Who set me up for these...), and about losing one's way.

In this entry I will describe how I for the first time had a direct experience of my own thought processes, discovering how they influenced my perception of reality.

Finding the traces

It was 1991, and I felt confused, alone and felt like I had completely lost track of where I wanted to go.

When reading The Bull and His Herdsman, and continuing with the second picture, I realized that I maybe was not completely lost – I had learned a lot, and I had seen many traces of the "other" reality I was searching for, even if this mostly was in the form of brief intuitive insights, or unexpected positive reactions from people.

The following poem inspired me to continue my search, even though it felt like each answer to a question led to many more new questions.

Many wrong paths cross where the dead tree stands by the rock.

Stairway Lars Gimstedt

> *Restlessly running round and round,*
> *in his stuffy nest of grass,*
>
> *Does he know his own error? In his search,*
> *just when his feet follow the traces,*
>
> *He has passed the bull by and has let him escape.*

I finalized my training at Psychosynthesis Palo Alto. A year before the final exam we were allowed to start working with training clients, and I rented a small office in downtown Seattle where I worked a couple of hours a week, at the same time working full time as an engineer at Boeing.

My new psychological knowledge and skills were acknowledged as useful in the management training program my employer had enrolled me in. The program led to a change of direction in my career at Boeing, from being a technical expert to middle manager. People of course knew about my other "professional leg", but as I used to joke about this at times – *"Training to become a psychotherapist is of course overkill as management training, but it is certainly useful…"*

Both working as a manager and as a psychotherapist made me more and more aware of how people's thought patterns form the reality they perceive.
I learned, on a very concrete level, that 99% of all conflicts in a work place come out of misunderstandings, out of people having thoughts

and beliefs about others, and out of poor ability to communicate in a straight-forward and honest way.

I also discovered, in my personal life, what my thoughts and beliefs about my divorce had led to: a very tense relationship with the mother of my children, where my attitude towards Anna was dominated by suspiciousness and bitterness.

On an intellectual level, and from my studies of ACIM, I realized that I should forgive Anna and let go of my grievances, in order to build my life up again, but on an emotional level this felt impossible. Each time we met, my bitterness, distrust and anger were activated.

I meditated on passages in ACIM that talked about forgiveness:

> *The world we see merely reflects our own internal frame of reference - the dominant ideas, wishes and emotions in our minds. "Projection makes perception" (Text, p. 445).*
>
> *We look inside first, decide the kind of world we want to see and then project that world outside, making it the truth as we see it. We make it true by our interpretations of what it is we are seeing. If we are using perception to justify our own mistakes – our anger, our impulses to attack, our lack of love in whatever form it may take – we will see a world of evil, destruction, malice, envy and despair.*
>
> *All this we must learn to forgive, not because we are being "good" and "charitable," but because*

what we are seeing is not true. We have distorted the world by our twisted defenses, and are therefore seeing what is not there. As we learn to recognize our perceptual errors, we also learn to look past them or "forgive." At the same time we are forgiving ourselves, looking past our distorted self-concepts to the Self That God created in us and as us.
(Introduction, "What it says".)

I trained my mind with the help of the following lessons:

Lesson 5.   I am never upset for the reason I think

Lesson 6.   I am upset because I see something that is not there.

Lesson 9.   I see nothing as it is now.

Lesson 21. I am determined to see things differently.

Lesson 24. I do not perceive my own best interests.

Lesson 33. There is another way of looking at the world.

Lesson 34. I could see peace instead of this.

I understood and accepted the message in the first six lessons in the list above. But when I arrived at Lesson 34, my whole mind revolted: *"What does He know about how it has been for me?"* Memories of deceit and lies, of selfishness and of unreasonable demands came up in my inner vision, making me be in the grip of deep bitterness and frustration.

A miracle

But then, the thought came: *"But, <u>Jesus</u> saw peace in the situations he met. With <u>worse</u> deceit, <u>bigger</u> lies, <u>far</u> more cruel treatment…"*

And I decided that before next time I would meet Anna, I would center myself by affirming *"I could see peace instead of this"*, until I felt calm

And I got to experience my first miracle: suddenly it felt like Anna listened, and for the first time we could suddenly talk with each other about what now was important – how we should arrange our lives in the best possible way for our children. And we reached agreements that I did not feel forced me to concessions or unreasonable compromises, agreements I felt I could support with all my heart. And I sensed that she regarded our agreements in the same way.

I suddenly understood, not only on an intellectual level, but on an *experiential* level, the "Miracle Principle" no 34 in ACIM:

> *"Miracles restore the mind to its fullness.
> By atoning for lack they establish perfect protection.*

> *The spirit's strength leaves no room for intrusions."*

And the miracle repeated itself in our contacts, even if it did not feel as overwhelming as the first time. Sometimes we both fell back into our old destructive patterns, and my anger bubbled up, but then I reminded myself: *"I could see peace instead of this"*, and my emotions subsided, I could just let go of my feelings of bitterness, and after a moment I could again listen and talk calmly.

Also in my job at the development department, which had its conflicts, intrigues and friction between people, as in most other work places, I could "rise above the battle field" and look at what was happening in a new way, thereby also reacting differently. Not so anybody noticed anything special, but many of my superiors and co-workers started to comment on my ability in getting people to talk *with* each other instead of *about* each other, in leading people quarrelling in meetings over to having constructive and honest discussions, in influencing angry and bitter persons to start to see things from more than one perspective.

I felt that a genuine inner change was taking place in me, even if I realized that it was only a beginning. But it still gave me hope: change was possible without having to "work with it". Many of my therapist colleagues used to say that true inner change was only possible if one activated a lengthy "inner transformation process". But ACIM stated clearly, that inner change can be the result of just *wanting* to see things in a new way, and by accepting Inner Guidance.

It felt like the text after the second image of The Bull and His Herdsman described me:

> *Reading the Sutras and listening to the teachings, the herdsman had an inkling of their message and meaning. He has discovered the traces.*
>
> *Now he knows that however varied and manifold, yet all things are of the one gold, and that his own nature does not differ from that of any other.*
>
> *But he cannot yet distinguish between what is genuine and what fake, still less between the true and the false. He can thus not enter the gate, and only provisionally can it be said that he has found the traces.*

A new family

Years passed, and I started to feel well established both in my role as a manager and as a therapist. My children had reached mid-adolescence, the result of which was that despite living most of the time with their mother, neither she or I saw much of them – their lives circled around friends, hobbies and different activities of their own.

I met a woman, Hi'ilani. We shared dedication to ACIM, and she felt like a "soul mate". Hi'ilani was native Hawaiian, and her name means "Held in the arms of heaven".

We soon moved together and created a new home. After a few more years I had a new family, and was again the father of two small children. I discovered I had grown into being a somewhat different father to these two than I had been with my older ones. Twenty years earlier I had had many principles and firm beliefs about raising children, and I had been firm but often extremely unreasonable.

I found myself now be a better listener, I found that I could establish a relationship with both Hi'ilani and our children that was characterized by presence and authenticity. We could almost always live in a harmonious way, and when conflicts arose, we could handle them gracefully with no residual bitterness or unresolved misunderstandings.

Next step

Coming to the year of 2002, I had now participated in two major airplane projects at Boeing, and in the second one we had passed the stages of final design, construction and flight tests. I switched from design office manager to customer support manager, and now became involved with training customers, and building up after-market activities.

But I felt that "the therapist" in me longed to get more space, and I started to nourish the thought of leaving my corporate career after thirty years. Most of my manager colleagues thought I was crazy, when I discussed this with them, but at the same time I felt that they also understood that I talked about some kind of life dream.

I started to "plant seeds" when talking with my superiors, about doing something completely different in my life. They first tried to persuade me to just back down to a role like senior adviser, which most of other manager coming near their sixties would do, letting life wind down in a nice and gentle way. But, they understood that these types of thoughts would not take root in me, and early 2003 we reached an agreement for a termination program, where my employer supported me financially in establishing my company, Psychosynthesis Forum, as a full time job. (I had registered the company already in 1991 in order to be able to work with clients.)

I felt anxious, of course, starting anew at the age of fifty-seven, even if I had worked part time with clients for ten years already. But I also felt strongly that deciding to do this meant that "I had found the traces" and that I now really had decided to follow them, wherever they might lead me.

Stairway Lars Gimstedt

Stairway　　　　　　　　　　　　　　　Lars Gimstedt

January 23, 2347. NSA Report.

****
NSA Report 2346-1001-3858
TOP SECRET. CLF code 0.
Department for The Transhuman Threat.
January 23 2347.
Unmonitored disappearances.
Case study TTT-JZ-1.
****

Since the start of this year, JZ has "travelled" extensively, visiting different Stairway Centers, meeting with individuals and groups. At each of these trips there has been a TSS disconnect and subsequent re-connect, and there is strong evidence that JZ has transported himself with some kind of neuroportation technique.

The present hypothesis is that there is another BQRF (Brainwave Quantum Resonance Field) aspect, where the field creates small time-space worm holes, through which the subject can instantaneously switch to a new location. On how the subject is able to select a location without fatal threats to survival, there is as yet no hypothesis at all, but our neurocontrol experts are working on this.

This ability, which now has been measured and documented better than before, even if it probably still involves a limited number of individuals, raises the security issue around JZ in an unprecedented way - we have now no way of containing him, or possibly others as well. Because of this fact, NSA-TTT is advocating maser blast termination of individuals posing Class Zero threats to the state, but we have not as yet got UN clearance for this. Other agencies share our view on this (See Appendix 1).

There is so far no viable scientific explanation for the neuroportation ability, despite the BQRF hypothesis, so high data stream probe surveillance of all individuals where TSS interrupts have been documented has been initiated. In addition to this, all Stairway documentation of JZ's and others movements and visits will be scanned.

The BQRF interpersonal influence hypothesis has since our last report been strengthened by psychological experiments at the NSA Neurocontrol Lab. These experiments that indicate that BQRF impact is dependent on the sender's emotional state, and that accepting, releasing and letting go of strong emotions of the type that create long term emotional states, like moods or depressions, have been shown to enhance the impact effect of BQRF. These effects were particularly strong when the emotions were bitterness, seeing oneself as a victim, or hate.

In his last blog entry (January 19) JZ also describes an incident, where he without knowing it, most probably exerted BQRF influence on his ex-wife, at the instant that he thought of forgiveness.

There seems to be little logical reason for him to forgive in the way he described, as his ex-wife had done nothing to improve their strained relation, but it seems like the very act of forgiveness was the neurological trigger for increasing BQRF activity. As for JZ himself, he had previously done nothing to make his ex believe that he would be prepared to act in any different or more positive way. There is no other reasonable explanation for her obvious change of emotional state, than sub-conscious BQRF influence exerted by JZ.

Even if the outcome of this BQRF interaction in this case was experienced as positive by both parties, it does not exclude the fact that BQRT could very well be used in aggressive ways. On the other hand, the fact that emotions like aggression, even if held sub-consciously, could inhibit the BQRF effect, makes it necessary to investigate this further. The experiments at the Neurocontrol lab will therefore continue.

****
End of NSA Report 2346-1001-3858
TOP SECRET. CLF code 0.
January 23 2347.
****

Stairway   Lars Gimstedt

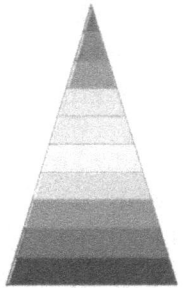

January 30, 2347.
Stairway New Zealand News.

Dear Sisters and Brothers

John says in his blog entry January 19 that he plans to visit all the Centers, and many have asked me when he will visit us. Sorry to say, I haven't heard of any specific plans, but I will inform you as soon as we know.

The NSA agents have been visiting us, with warrants to go through our material, and this has taken up a lot of my time. This stresses the point of holding this newsletter confidential, and I ask you all to keep them in a safe place.

They of course wondered about the ancient photo-copier, but we told them we use it in our children groups' history lessons.

Stairway

Lars Gimstedt

~.~. * .~.~

When John writes about how he started to understand how the mind and the ego make us value and judge others, how he started to "find the traces", we have to remember that at that time these concepts were quite new, and the knowledge about how the subconscious mind works was not as spread as it is today. After all, mankind has known about ACIM for more than three hundred years now, and it has become a natural part of our culture, whereas John and his contemporaries had known ACIM only for forty years. Even psychology, a natural part of our basic education now, had only been known for a sole hundred years, and was not common knowledge at all.

Nevertheless, I can relate to the stage "finding the traces". For me, my adolescence was very dominated by a negative self-image, making me believe that others were all the time judging me, evaluating me, and finding me not worthy of their acceptance, respect or love.

But, with the help of ACIM, for example by reading lesson 69,

Stairway Lars Gimstedt

"My grievances hide the light of the world in me",

I could finally forgive the ones that I thought were "condemning" me. And in doing this, I "found the traces" of my ego's thought processes – by believing that people judged me, I subconsciously judged <u>them</u>. And as long as I continued to do this, I could not really see them.

And by "hiding my light", they could not really see me...

"You have no idea of the tremendous release and deep peace that comes from meeting yourself and your brothers totally without judgment. When you recognize what you are and what your brothers are, you will realize that judging them in any way is without meaning. In fact, their meaning is lost to you precisely <u>because</u> you are judging them. All uncertainty comes from the belief that you are under the coercion of judgment."
(T-3.VI.3)

Until next time, with love

Lena Adamson

~.~.~.~. * .~.~.~.~

March 23, 2347.
BLOG ENTRY: Finding the Bull – Skill.

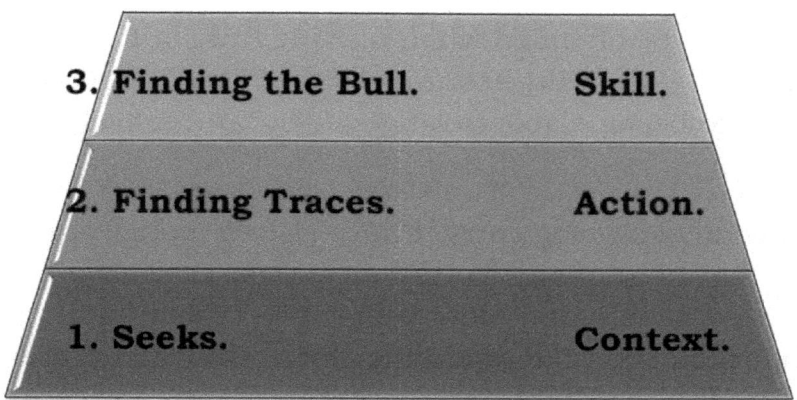

Welcome back to John Zacharias' blog.

The TSS people have asked me to participate in meetings for discussing NSA's investigation of myself and of the Stairway Movement, and I have attended a few meetings, where I met both TSS officials and experts from their Neurocontrol Lab (which I did not know it existed before).

They revealed their theory of neurological remote influencing of others and of neurological impact on the time-space matrix, which they called Brainwave Quantum Resonance Field. I think they wanted to get some clues from me about things we in Stairway describe as miracles. I tried in vain to explain to them that a miracle is a transformation of the mind, and I explained the phenomenon of psychological projection of mental content, creating a seemingly real world, but I think they regarded me as having a psychological disorder…

It is amusing, and I feel both compassion and I get impressed, when I listen to the frantic inventiveness of the ego. How it can invent anything, increasingly complicated, in order to preserve its world. (They will probably be offended when reading this, but I hope they will accept my assurances that I really wish for them to become able to let go of fear and to feel peace.)

Since my last blog entry, I have visited more Centers, and have had many fruitful meetings. There is a lot going on, more and more people I have met have shown a deep understanding of the Atonement, and of the Power of True Forgiveness.

Back to my own path

To continue the story about my own Path: it was 2003, and I had started to work full time as a psychotherapist.

I managed to sign an agreement with a corporate health-care company with offices in most of the towns of Washington, and I started to work for them a couple of days per week. Doing this, I quickly found that my usual therapeutic techniques did not work well in my new role as "behaviorist counsellor". The reason for this was that the companies sending their employees to us limited the counselling to three or four sessions only, whereas I before had usually worked with clients over longer periods of time.

Stairway Lars Gimstedt

I searched for more efficient therapy methods, which led me into taking courses in Cognitive Behavioral Therapy (CBT) and Neurolinguistic Programming (NLP). With the new tools from these psychological schools, I could now soon help people to achieve real change already after a few sessions.

This inspired me to again start to reflect on the psychological change I had gone through myself over the last ten years. Much of this change had to do with my accepting the idea that we do not see reality in an objective way. We create inner mental images of reality, and then we project these images outwards so that we perceive them outside of ourselves, "seeing" them as our "true" external reality.

I also started to reflect on my spiritual development, which felt like it had leveled out somewhat the last couple of years.

Through my studies of cognitive psychology and my experiences from applying this knowledge in my work, I had become increasingly aware of the fact that psychological change does not only come out of becoming aware of the influence of one's context, and how one reacts to it. Long term psychological growth is primarily the result of developing *new skills*. Both improving those one have, and developing completely new ones. Awareness and insights are necessary for becoming *motivated* to change, but these do not by themselves lead to lasting change. Change is the result of *acting* in a new way and new ways of acting require self-awareness, motivation and new *skills*.

And I asked myself – if this was true for psychological and personal growth, should it not be true for spiritual growth as well?

I read the ACIM lessons again, and I now saw, with my new "Cognitive Psychology glasses" on, that the lessons could very well have been written by a Cognitive Psychology therapist: the goal of the lessons is to teach, and get the student to train, the ability of "True Perception", with which we can start to see that which points at Truth:

Lesson 91. Miracles are seen in light.
> *It is important to remember that miracles and vision necessarily go together. This needs repeating, and frequent repeating. It is a central idea in your new thought system, and the perception that it produces. The miracle is always there. Its presence is not caused by your vision; its absence is not the result of your failure to see. It is only your awareness of miracles that is affected. You will see them in the light; you will not see them in the dark.*

In the Bible Jesus is said to describe himself as "The Light of the world", which at first sight seems to describe Him as someone having divine abilities impossible for us to achieve. But he also said, according to John 14:12:

> *Very truly I tell you, whoever believes in me will do the works I have been doing, and they will do even greater things than these.*

And in ACIM He reinforces this, by asking us to affirm:

> *Lesson 62. Forgiveness is my function as the light of the world.*
>
> *Lesson 79. Let me recognize the problem so it can be solved.*

What do we need to become better at?

So it seemed to me: Jesus is telling us that we need to develop new skills, in order to become proficient in what he calls a Miracle Worker, in the service of God. But, I wondered, which *are* the skills one needs to develop, to be able to accept and take on this role, to accept one's own active part in The Atonement?

In my work as a psychotherapist I had often met patients suffering from various personality disturbances, in which they believed themselves to have "supernatural abilities", but where the ego had become inflated, making up exaggerated and often destructive beliefs about its abilities. Despite their high regard about themselves, and despite their often charismatic influence on others, these persons had often a poor ability for feeling compassion, and were often poor listeners. The underlying driving force seemed to be ego-inflation and a need of control and power.

I suspected that there were many others, seemingly well-adjusted in society, which through similar personality traits could have used their charisma and persuasive powers to have taken on roles like the guru, the sect leader, or similar. But despite their claims of being enlightened, these persons are seldom spiritually advanced at all – on the contrary their communication is based on the underlying message of the ego: *"The world is characterized by danger and lack. You have to defend what you have, and make sure you get what you need. Let me help you with this."*

I realized that the ego even in "normal", descent, good persons may, under the influence of such a hidden message, dominate their thoughts, making them influence others in the same destructive direction. When studying different blogs and email ads I could observe this tendency of ego-inflation in many New Age movements like "The Law of Attraction", "The Secret", "Avatar" and other similar to these.

So I posed myself the question: *"If I want to accept the role as the light of the world, and the role of the Miracle Worker, which skills do I need to develop? And how do I stop my ego from taking over?"*

During the time twenty years earlier in my life, when I was frantically searching for information on spiritual development, I among other books bought many books by Jiddu Krishnamurti, and I dug these books out again from my book crates.

Krishnamurti, in the recordings of his numerous seminars and in his books, talks a lot about the importance of observing the thinking process itself, without judging or evaluating any specific thoughts, and about the importance of meditation as an indispensable tool for "hearing" the silence *beneath* the thinking process.

In one of books I found, "The Wholeness of Life", the following passage caught my eye:

> Meditation is the attention in which there is no registration. Normally the brain is registering almost everything, the noise, the words which are being used - it registering like a tape.
> Now is it possible for the brain not to register except that which is absolutely necessary? Why should I register an insult? Why?
> Why should I register flattery? It is unnecessary. Why should I register any hurts? Unnecessary. Therefore, register only that which is necessary in order to operate in daily life - as a technician, a writer and so on - but psychologically, do not register anything. In meditation there is no registration psychologically, no registration except the practical facts of living, going to the office, working in a factory and so on - nothing else. Out of that comes complete silence, because thought has come to an end - except to function only where it is absolutely necessary. Time has come to an end and there is a totally different kind of movement, in silence.

> Religion then has a totally different meaning, whereas before it was a matter of thought. Thought made the various religions and therefore each religion is fragmented and in each fragment there are multiple divisions. All that is called religion, including the beliefs, the hopes, the fears and the desire to be secure in another world and so on, is the result of thought. It is not religion, it is merely the

movement of thought, in fear, in hope, in trying to find security - a material process.

Then what is religion? *It is the investigation, with all one's attention, with the summation of all one's energy, to find that which is sacred, to come upon that which is holy.* That can only take place when there is freedom from the noise of thought - the ending of thought and time, psychologically, inwardly - but not the ending of knowledge in the world where you have to function with knowledge. That which is holy, that which is sacred, which is truth, can only be when there is complete silence, when the brain itself has put thought in its right place. Out of that immense silence there is that which is sacred.

Silence demands space, space in the whole structure of consciousness. There is no space in the structure of one's consciousness as it is, because it is crowded with fears - crowded, chattering, chattering. *When there is silence, there is immense, timeless space; then only there is a possibility of coming upon that which is the eternal, sacred.*

The first step: become aware of yourself.

I realized that the ability to meditate was *one* of the skills I needed to develop. And then not the ability or discipline to meditate certain periods of time during the day, rather the ability to find a meditative state of mind whenever I needed it, especially whilst interacting with other people.

As my meditation technique, I just used a simple breathing exercise (which I later presented on my web site under the name the AOM Breathing). Every time I encountered a difficulty around interacting with people, I would use the AOM technique a couple of seconds, at the same time reminding myself about the ACIM lesson of the day, or simply asking myself *"What would Jesus had said or done now?"*

I immediately found that this simple method made wonders, sometimes even miracles – the way I saw "difficult" persons changed immediately into looking at them with compassion and a sense of inner calm: *"Just now, there is no hurry. Just listen, and see what unfolds."*

And my old instinctive reactions started to change into acting in new, more constructive, ways, even if I had many "fallbacks" to my "old autopilot".

And when I failed, I no longer blamed myself. I changed calling these incidents "failures" or "mistakes" into instead calling them "feedback": my actions always give outcomes, and these represent either positive or negative feedback. In the latter case, I could then just ask myself: *"This was not the outcome I wanted. What could a better way of acting be next time this happens?"* And if my conscious or my subconscious mind did not help me with this, I would continue by asking *"What would Jesus want me to do?"*

I often reminded myself of the beautiful passage in ACIM (T-8:III.4):

> *When you meet anyone, remember it is a holy encounter.*
>
> *As you see him you will see yourself.*
>
> *As you treat him you will treat yourself.*
>
> *As you think of him you will think of yourself.*
>
> *Never forget this, for in him you will find yourself or lose yourself.*

And I also reminded myself about ACIM describing the world as "a learning device", where everything that happens is a new opportunity for stopping oneself in order to become aware of one's thought patterns, and then for asking for guidance from one's Higher I, one's Self, one's Inner Guide, The Holy Spirit, or whatever one calls the Truth that resides within us all.

The second step: choose again.

In this inner process, that needs to become an automatic habit, I realized that the most important point is what ACIM asks us to do: "*Choose again.*"

I realized, when practicing new ways of acting and reacting, that the crucial thing is *choice*. Choosing whether to listen to one's ego or to listen to The Inner Voice of God.

ACIM stresses this need for conscious choice strongly:

> *Be Vigilant Only for God and His Kingdom.*
>
> *We said before that the Holy Spirit is evaluative,*

and must be. He sorts out the true from the false in your mind, and teaches you to judge every thought you allow to enter it in the light of what God put there.

Whatever is in accord with this light He retains, to strengthen the Kingdom in you. What is partly in accord with it He accepts and purifies. But what is out of accord entirely He rejects by judging against.

This is how He keeps the Kingdom perfectly consistent and perfectly unified. Remember, however, that what the Holy Spirit rejects the ego accepts. This is because they are in fundamental disagreement about everything, being in fundamental disagreement about what you are.

The ego's beliefs on this crucial issue vary, and that is why it promotes different moods.

The Holy Spirit never varies on this point, and so the one mood He engenders is joy. He protects it by rejecting everything that does not foster joy, and so He alone can keep you wholly joyous.

(T-6.V.C.1)

Third step: persistent practice.

Everything I have described above soon became strong insights that then grew into strong beliefs.

But, to my dismay, even believing strongly did not by itself lead to permanent inner change. Even if my interactions with most people became more and more harmonious, my old "spine reactions" could still be triggered at home, with my family.

My wife could say things that reminded me of painful experiences in our mutual past, and I could become flooded by memories of incidents where I had felt powerless, confused, belittled, misunderstood. This could put me in an inner state dominated by frustration and anger, and I could lash out.

My kids could behave badly, ignoring my attempts to correct them, and subconscious memories from my own childhood of repression, not feeling seen, feeling psychologically abused, etcetera, were activated. And sometimes these memories triggered intense anger with subconscious and unresolved guilt underneath, and I could lash out, saying things that really hurt, things I afterwards bitterly regretted having said.

So I practiced hard to stop myself. I realized that anger, being an emotion and therefore being built up by different processes in my body like heart rate, blood pressure, adrenaline, and so on, has a duration in time that one cannot alter. I realized that when I became blocked by a strong emotion, the smartest thing I could do was to take a time-out.

I learned to just say *"We need to talk, but first I need to be for myself a short moment"* or something similar, and then go somewhere where I could sit down and do my AOM breathing, until the emotion had resided.

And also to ask myself "*What do I really want to happen now?*"

In the beginning this could take rather long time, and the child involved could sometimes open the door and ask cautiously "*Is the anger over yet?*" and I could just answer "*No, not yet, but soon. Wait until I come out.*"

But after a while, with persistent practice, the time for calming myself became shorter and shorter, until it finally sufficed to just take a deep breath, and to start the interaction over, from the beginning.

Finding the Bull

In hindsight, I would say that this learning process took another seven years. When arriving at approximately the year of 2010, I had, using the symbol of The Bull and His Herdsman, "found the bull". That is, I had learned to become aware of my old thought processes, dominated by my ego, and on a psychological level I had learned to stop myself from acting by instinct.

I had started to realize that my ego is not really working in my best interest, despite it emphatically claims it does.

And I had started to open myself up to the thought that something else deep inside *knows* my best interest, which also is the best interest of all others involved.

But I also realized, that becoming aware and starting to act on the awareness is not the same thing as having solved the problem. As one of the poems beneath the third picture in The Bull says:

On seeing the bull and hearing his bellow,

Tai-sung, the painter, surpassed his craft.

*Accurately he pictured the heart-bull
from head to tail,*

*And yet, on carefully looking,
he is not yet quite complete.*

I had started to see glimpses of my True Mind, and I had started to see the fundamental difference between this and the ego. I had started to realize that there is no way of reconciling these two, rather there is the need of actively choosing Right-mindedness whenever ego thoughts come.

But, I also understood that even if I had achieved a lot on a psychological level, on a spiritual level I was still stuck in perceiving the world as "real". Even if I had "taken back" many of my own psychological projections on it, I still experienced the physical world and myself as reality.

Stairway Lars Gimstedt

March 27, 2347. NSA Report.

****

NSA Report 2346-1001-3916
TOP SECRET. CLF code 0.
Department for The Transhuman Threat.
March 27 2347.
Unmonitored disappearances.
Case study TTT-JZ-1.

****

JZs latest blog entry has confirmed the hypothesis about BQRF and its connection to mind training techniques, and how he using these techniques could start influencing others' subconscious minds.

It seems that conscious control of one's own mind is the key to actually starting to control the Brainwave Quantum Resonance Field BQRF.

It also seems like JZ was starting to have this control as far back in time as 2010, but that it was also at this time he started to become victim of the "split mind delusion", which he later on would reinforce in others via the Stairway movement, alienating more and more people from realistic and sound scientific thought patterns.

So, even if BQRF is a powerful tool, that science really has to understand and learn to control, and that could be put to good use, JZ and others have been using BQRF in destructive ways, causing delusion and confusion.

JZ's travelling to the different Stairway centers has continued and in an increasing rate – during March he visited one every third day. Each time there was a TSS disconnect, and now the automatic reconnect has taken longer and longer time. In the last two cases, the reconnect took 36 hours.

This increase is very disturbing, and could be a sign of that JZ has started to achieve an ability to actually control the radiation fields from the RPNE transmitters (Remote Positron Neurologic Emission). If this ability spreads to more individuals, it would constitute an unprecedented breach of national security. NSA-TTT strongly advocates maser blast termination, in cases where individuals use this new ability for example to enter restricted government locations.

****

End of NSA Report 2346-1001-3916
TOP SECRET. CLF code 0.
March 27 2347.

****

Stairway   Lars Gimstedt

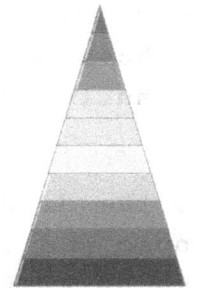

March 30, 2347.
Stairway New Zealand News.

Dear Sisters and Brothers

One of our members, who is active in a group studying morphogenetic fields and psychic abilities, asked me why John seemed to dismiss the TSS agents' idea of BQRF, Brainwave Quantum Resonance Field, as "amusing".

I could not answer him, but promised to forward the question via com message to John and to return with his response. As psychic ability is a topic often brought up in our monthly meetings, I have chosen to report on John's answer here, for all of you to reflect on.

John answered via a com video call, and it was really exciting to talk with him like this in person! He looks really very old, but seems to be "young in mind", and he is very easy-going. I was of course very nervous first, but his gentle ways and his sense of humor made me soon relax.

I hope I understood him correctly, but this is how I interpreted what he explained to me:

BQRF, and any other forms of psychic abilities, may or may not work. But, as everything in our physical reality, visible or invisible, all these manifestations have <u>form</u>, and so by definition they do not belong to Truth, which is without form.

By themselves, psychic abilities are neutral, like our body and our thoughts. The only important thing is what we use them for, what our purpose is. If a person having developed an ability like this brings it to The Holy Spirit to use, the psychic ability <u>can</u> be helpful in helping others awaken. But if it is used by the ego, the ability will revert to mere magic, which might be impressing, but which will just reinforce the ego's grip over the mind.

So what John said had amused him, was not that BQRF was "false" or "non-existent", but that it was an impressing example of what the mind can <u>manufacture</u>, in contrast to what God <u>creates</u>. What the mind can make up in the world of form can be, and very often is, impressing in its complexity and ingenuity, and it is always logically consistent. But this does not alter the fundamental fact that it still belongs to the domain of form, and is therefore illusionary.

After talking with John, I scanned ACIM for the word "purpose", and immediately found ACIM's answer to this issue:

> "The test of everything on earth is simply this; 'What is it for?' The answer makes it what it is for you. It has no meaning of itself, yet you can give reality to it, according to the purpose that you serve."
> (T-24.VII.6.)

~.~. * .~.~

About the story of John's Path:

He found that the skill he needed to develop, in the stage of his awaking he was in then, was the ability to go into a meditative state.

Stairway — Lars Gimstedt

Reading this felt like a very important reminder for me — I realized how easy it is to become caught in everyday business.

He described the process of training this skill as

1. Become aware of yourself.
2. Choose again.
3. Persistent practice.

The three steps John describes make it sound simple, but even with my limited experience of meditation, I know how difficult it is, and how important the third step really is. But also the first is crucial, without this, nothing will happen. And again, without actively choosing (ego or God), ego will surely take over, due to our "automatic" sub-conscious conditioning.

For me personally, I don't really know whether I have, as John describes it, "found the Bull". Sometimes it feels as I have, but other times I realize after something negative has happened in my interaction with someone, that I "lost it again"…

It was comforting to read, that it took <u>him</u> seven years to turn his insights into a reliable and persistent habit.

ACIM also reminds us about how important it is to not only understand and get insights, but to actively form new habits:

> "The <u>habit</u> of engaging with God and His creations is easily made if you <u>actively</u> refuse to let your mind slip away.
> The problem is not one of concentration; it is the belief that no one, including yourself, is worth consistent effort. Side with me consistently against this deception, and do not permit this shabby belief to pull you back.
> The disheartened are useless to themselves and to me, but only the ego can be disheartened."
> (T-4.IV.7)

Until next time, with love

Lena Adamson

~.~.~.~. * .~.~.~.~

May 18, 2347.
BLOG ENTRY: Catching the Bull – Reality.

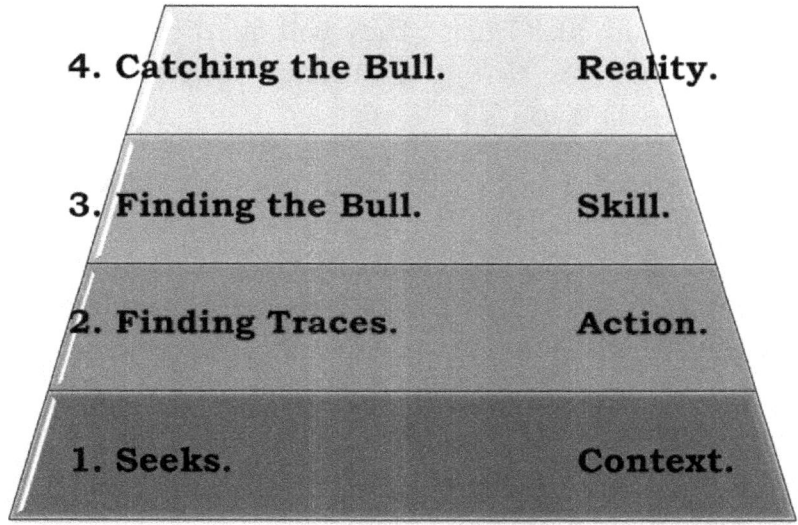

Welcome back to my blog, the blog of John Zacharias.

Since my last entry I have visited twenty more centers. I am glad to hear that new members have been signing up in an increasing rate, all over the world.

I do not know whether it is my activities that have contributed to this, or if it is NSA's increased surveillance, but it doesn't matter. We both seem to contribute in making more and more people to reflect on themselves and their perception of the world.

NSA seem to have become very disturbed by the increasing number of people causing disconnects in the probe surveillance, and I think that everyone of us communicating with their agents should try to

Stairway   Lars Gimstedt

convince them that there is no "evil" plan behind this, it is only a natural effect of more and more true Right-mindedness, and that those attaining this ability constitute no risk whatsoever to anyone. (I am sure they read this, and I hope they will open themselves up to the fact that threat or attack in any form is completely alien to us.)

I have received much feed-back about my description of my own path to awakening, both when visiting centers and in com messages. Many have said that they have re-read "A Stairway to Heaven", and that they have understood it on a deeper level, when they now know more about how my life history was before and whilst writing the book.

Many have told me how they have been involved with the Stairway Movement and how they have studied ACIM for a long time, but that when they read what I wrote about how change does not follow from insights and beliefs only, and started to practice the lessons with more discipline, something new started to happen. A few of these have reported complete transformation of perception, and they told me that a thorough re-reading of the ACIM text had been the most important thing for them, as it made them more receptive to the lessons.

Many, especially younger persons, find the lessons easier to pursue as a daily practice than reading the Textbook, but I really want to emphasize this last thing in what I wrote above about the feedback I got: in order to fully wake up to Right-mindedness and to True Perception, it is necessary to read the text carefully. The message is far more radical than most people realize, and a thorough understanding of the Textbook is necessary for the lessons to work well.

Re-discovery

This connects in a natural way in continuing my story about my own Path.

In 2013, 27 years had passed by since I first read ACIM. Reading it had made me change my professional career from being a scientist and development engineer to becoming a psychotherapist.

During my twenty years of working with Psychosynthesis, I had opened myself up to the notion of a Higher I, the Self, and to the spiritual realm. But, I had more and more focused on the *psychological* side, concentrating on my own personal development, and concentrating on learning and developing methods for helping others with their personal growth.

During the year of 2013 I had finalized the documentation of my working methods for personal growth and mind-training, and had "productified" most of these in the form of e-courses on the website of my company, PsychosynthesisForum.com.

The last e-course I put together up to then was named My Mission, and was the first of approximately twenty e-courses on my web site, where I for the first time had introduced an openly spiritual agenda.

But when I, after the release of My Mission, thought about what to do next in terms of publishing things

Stairway Lars Gimstedt

on the web site, I happened to read something I had written a long time before in my Psychosynthesis Forum blog (psychosynthesisforum.blogspot.se):

Different paths to the goal

With the image below I try to illustrate that the ways through these levels of development can be very different for different persons, and that there is no "right way" or "wrong way", as long as it leads towards the "Goal" (symbolized by the sun in the image).

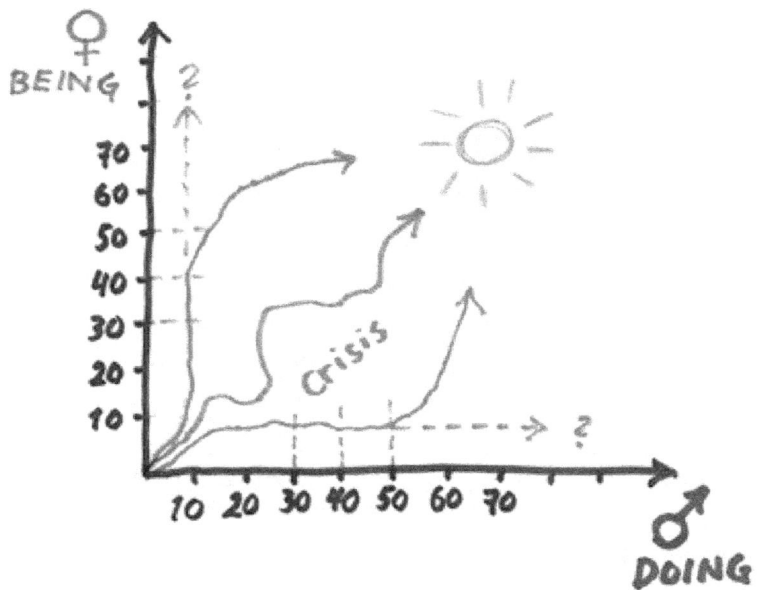

The lower curve represents a typical development path of a person in the industrialized countries, where there is a strong focus on personal and professional development. This path usually feels OK, up to the point where the person starts to feel "*I am no longer coming nearer my life goal*" (=the sun in the picture, that stands for our deepest life goal).

Or the feeling does not come expressed in words, but more

as a sense of meaninglessness, spleen, depression, etc. This is sometimes experienced as periods of crisis. These typically come every tenth year after the age of 30.

When they happen, some "press harder on the accelerator", investing more energy, but on "more of the same", as change of job, new car or new partner... Which usually leads to an even larger sense of meaninglessness. Others, on the other hand, "listen" to their crisis, and activate their spiritual development (the curve bends upwards), and a sense of meaningfulness starts to re-emerge.

The upper curve represents those that early in life identify with the spiritual realm. This usually also feels good, up to the point in mid-life when a paradoxical feeling of meaninglessness starts to emerge also for persons in this category, with similar words - "*despite the fact that this path should have led me to my deepest goal, it doesn't.*" And furthermore, life does not work well on a practical level, like income, a home, relations, etc.

If this person now persists with "more of the same" it often leads to a sense of resignation, cynicism, depression, etc. But, if this person takes his or her crisis seriously, and takes hold of his or her *personal* and professional development, new possibilities will open.

And the curve in the middle may stand for most of us, where it goes up and down, back and forth...

The morale of this description is
that <u>both</u> personal and spiritual development are necessary in order to become a whole person, one that is able to embrace both Doing and Being, that is able to express both one's masculine and one's feminine side, that is able to unite Jin and Jang.

> And, the paradox is that, in order to be able to let go of one's ego, one *first* has to develop a strong, self-aware and stable ego. And this is valid for the Self as well.

And when reading the last sentence, I somehow knew that the first part of my own mission was finalized, and that I should now return to the core of it. I had even stated my Mission on the top of each one of my web pages: Find your Self, without being aware of the fact that this really was something I was telling myself to do.

And I realized that a circle had closed, and I felt a strong urge to focus completely again on my "original trigger" for my life path change, A Course in Miracles, instead as just having it as my own personal reference base.

Back to the Re-source

I re-read ACIM's textbook once more, and started to do the lessons, now for the third time. I could feel that I read much of it as if I had never read it before; my twenty years of working as a psychotherapist made me see much of ACIM differently compared to when I first read it, back in 1986.

This led me to compile an e-course about ACIM, "A Psychosynthesis Perspective on A Course in Miracles", that I published at the end of the year 2013. I presented this course as a complement to ACIM, primarily offered to "ACIM students" who also had a general interest in modern psychology and a specific interest in Psychosynthesis and cognitive methods.

Stairway — Lars Gimstedt

I published the course in a preliminary version, inviting people to help me complete the course by joining discussion groups that I also offered, both as groups meeting in Seattle, and as groups communicating via Skype Video Conference (an early primitive fore-runner to today's VR holographic conference).

As I mentioned above, I read the lessons with "new eyes". For example I experienced these ones saying something different from my original interpretation:

> Lesson 91.   Miracles are seen in light.
>
> Lesson 97.   I am spirit.
>
> Lesson 106.   Let me be still
> and listen to the truth.

I had understood long before that it is necessary to "be vigilant for God's Kingdom" in choosing the Self instead of choosing the ego, to ensure that one's core value base is in line with Right-mindedness.

But I now realized that this statement, and the message conveyed in the lessons above, really are more radical compared to how I had interpreted them: it is necessary to choose, *in each and every moment of time*, which we want to allow constituting reality in our mind: the physical world or the Real World.

Discipline and persistence

In leading the discussion groups that soon were formed, I encountered a lot of people that longed for Heaven but subconsciously also wanted to keep

Earth. They tried to do this by "spiritualizing" things in the physical world, like compassion, love, nature, beauty, fine arts, music, and so on.

Even if this helped in shifting focus from fear to love, and gave positive "vibrations", the "spiritualizing" tendency still kept them trapped in the thought system of the ego.

As one of the poems beneath the fourth picture of The Bull and His Herdsman says:

> *With great effort the herdsman succeeded*
> *in catching the bull.*
>
> *But stubborn, wilful and strong,*
> *this bull is not easily gentled!*
>
> *At times he breaks out and climbs up*
> *to the high plains*
>
> *Or rushes down into foggy marshlands*
> *to hide himself there.*

Stairway

I meditated, over a long period of time, on this image and on the text underneath the picture:

> *For the first time he encountered the bull that for so long had been hiding in the wilderness.*
>
> *But this pleasantly familiar wilderness still attracts the bull strongly. He yearns for the sweet-smelling grass and is difficult to hold.*
>
> *Stubborn self-will rages in him and wild animal-nature rules him. If the herdsman wants to make the bull really gentle, he must discipline him with the whip.*

I did not really want to use "the whip" on my friends in the discussion groups, but I felt that if I wanted to become a genuine Miracle Worker, if I wanted to be of true service, I needed to use "the whip" on myself.

My whip

I felt strongly that discovering and "seeing" one's split mind is a good beginning, an opening towards something new. But I also understood that it was not enough to be able to acquire what ACIM calls "true perception", for example in the section "Miracles as True Perception":

> *I have stated that the basic concepts referred to in this course are not matters of degree. Certain fundamental concepts cannot be understood in terms of opposites.*

> *It is impossible to conceive of light and darkness or everything and nothing as joint possibilities. They are all true or all false.*
>
> *It is essential that you realize your thinking will be erratic until a firm commitment to one or the other is made.*
> *(T-3.II.1)*

But where and how to find this "whip"?

ACIM is a mind training course, and for me as a psychologist it was tempting to use ACIM as a tool to become more and more skilled in identifying problems and finding good solutions for them. My former background as a development engineer was of course also involved in this type of thinking.

But ACIM reminded me, in many places both in the text, in the lessons and in the manual, that to experience "a holy instant", in which one sees with True Perception, one cannot and really *should not* rely purely on one's own abilities:

> *The holy instant is the result of your determination to be holy. It is the answer. The desire and the willingness to let it come precede its coming. You prepare your mind for it only to the extent of recognizing that you want it above all else.*
>
> *It is not necessary that you do more; indeed, it is necessary that you realize that <u>you cannot do more</u>. Do not attempt to give the Holy Spirit what He does not ask, or you will add the ego to Him*

and confuse the two. He asks but little.
(T18.IV.1)

Jesus even warns about becoming the victim of ego-inflation, exaggerating one's own importance:

> *The healer who relies on his own readiness is endangering his understanding.*
>
> *You are perfectly safe as long as you are completely unconcerned about your readiness, but maintain a consistent trust in mine.*
> *(T2:V.4)*

So I ultimately realized that my "whip" had to be reminding myself constantly, that I *never* know what is best for me or for others. And at the same time affirming *my willingness* to be guided in what to do, and then just listen inwards, opening myself up to the Holy Spirit, the Voice of God that He placed in each of us at the instant of the Fall, when we erroneously believed that we were cast out from Paradise.

The thought of "surrendering" to someone else's direction made my ego revolt, but at the same time I felt a paradoxical feeling of security when I chose this passage in ACIM as my daily "mantra":

> *You can do much on behalf of your own healing and that of others if, in a situation calling for help, you think of it this way:*
>
> *I am here only to be truly helpful.*
>
> *I am here to represent Him Who sent me.*

> *I do not have to worry about what to say or what to do, because He Who sent me will direct me.*
>
> *I am content to be wherever He wishes, knowing He goes there with me.*
>
> *I will be healed as I let Him teach me to heal.*
>
> *(T2-V:A.18)*

I realized that there is really no conflict between developing new skills and at the same time let go of believing that *I* know how to solve an interpersonal problem. By instead believing firmly in The Holy Spirit's ability to decide what I should do, I let Him <u>use</u> my skills. Better to be a <u>skilled</u> Miracle Worker than an unskilled one...

Another passage I also found useful as a "whip" for "catching my mind", stopping it from "bolting back into the wilderness" of the ego, was the following instruction (from ACIM T-30:I.1):

> *1) Today I will make no decisions by myself.*
>
> *2) If I make no decisions by myself, this is the day that will be given me.*
>
> *3) I have no question. I forgot what to decide.*

4) At least I can decide I do not like what I feel now.

5) And so I hope I have been wrong.

6) I want another way to look at this.

7) Perhaps there is another way to look at this. What can I lose by asking?

Seeing another reality

So, every time I experienced emotions like irritation, discontent, anger, fear, or I felt criticized, felt controlled by someone, I felt impatience with someone, I reminded myself: *"I don't know anything, but I don't like this feeling. I hope I am wrong, and I really want to see this differently. What do You want me to do?"*

And more and more often, I "caught my Bull", and stopped my ego from charging ahead, and the negative emotion subsided, and changed into a sometimes paradoxical feeling of inner peace (paradoxical because the situation might not be peaceful at all). I found myself doing something completely different from my usual reactions, like just listening, or asking for clarification, or just touching the person without saying anything.

And my perception of my "reality" changed, which made me aware that what I used to "see" before;

things I *would* "see" if I failed to "catch my Bull", were in reality things I had made up myself and then projected outwards, onto others.

Instead of hearing what I formerly could have interpreted as an attack on myself, I could now hear a call for help.

Inviting the miracle

I was amazed at how just reminding oneself of one's *willingness* to see differently could change things so rapidly; sometimes it really felt like miracles had started to happen.

In my role as a psychotherapist, I had often helped people let go of their negative emotions with different release techniques, which were helpful, but that felt much slower and inefficient compared to this. But, I also recognized that part of what I had taught my clients was still relevant, and could be applied into "welcoming the miracle" as well.

I went back and reviewed material I had produced, and discovered that I had even made charts of different levels of negative feelings, where I had described what they do to our thought patterns, our self-image and or inner image of God:

Level	Emotion	Thought	Self-image	Image of God
PRIDE	Arrogance	Conceit	Demanding	Indifferent
ANGER	Hate	Aggression	Antagonistic	Unforgiving
DESIRE	Lust	Dependence	A failure	Rejecting
FEAR	Anxiety	Avoidance	Insecure	Judging
SORROW	Regret	Pessimism	Tragic	Uncaring
APATHY	Despair	Resignation	Hopeless	Punishing
GUILT	Guilty	Destructive	Evil	Avenging
SHAME	Humiliation	Withering	Hateful	Contemptuous

(From my e-course Release the Emotion from 2007.)

And in the context of the path of awakening that I now had consciously made a decision to continue to walk, I could see from the corresponding image about levels of positive emotions (shown below), that I had now reached the level "Will" – *wanting* to see differently, *wanting* to achieve True Perception.

And I was amazed by the fact that I already at that time, ten years earlier in my life, had described both the thought processes and the image of God in a way that felt like it matched the paradoxes I was experiencing now: when I stopped relying on myself only, and opened up to inner guidance, my thought process became creative, and my experience of my Inner Guidance was Inspiration.

Stairway   Lars Gimstedt

Level	Emotion	Thought proc.	Self-image	Image of God
ILLUMINATION	(Indescribable)	Presence	I Am	I Am
PEACE	Bliss	Enlightenment	I am perfect	In everything
HAPPINESS	Joy	Transformation	I am whole	Embracing
LOVE	Love	Revelation	I am kind	Loving
REASON	Empathy	Abstraction	I am needed	Wise
ACCEPTANCE	Forgiveness	Transcendence	I am human	Compassionate
WILL	**Optimism**	**Creation**	**I want**	**Inspiring**
NEUTRALITY	Trust	Tolerance	I am OK	Creative
COURAGE	Firmness	Observance	I am growing	Allowing

Co-creation

My changed, and now more humble, attitude to my own "expertize" probably had an influence on the people attending my discussions groups as well, and more and more creative ideas from others found their way into the course "A Psychosynthesis Perspective on ACIM".

The e-course became my "best-seller", and I had to allocate more and more of my time to answering mail questions and to leading the discussion groups.

I started to feel ambivalent – on one hand I really wanted to help the ones using my material in their ACIM studies; on the other hand I wanted to give them more than just my day to day assistance.
I asked the Holy Spirit to guide me, and after a while I more and more felt that I should put together something that people could use by themselves, or as a material for their own ACIM discussion groups.
I therefore started to write a book in the fall of 2018, in which I tried to gather everything that quite

fragmented and unstructured had been put into the e-course.

2019 I devoted all my time to my new task, letting all the groups in Seattle and on the internet continue on their own.

Writing the book forced me to read the textbook of ACIM once again, and again I found "new things" I had not seen before. I became astonished that I could have forgotten what I now felt were crucial and central parts of the textbook, but I realized that my original memories of these parts probably did not match my changed way of perceiving reality, and had therefore been repressed, which in these cases was a good thing: I needed to read the texts with "new eyes".

I realized that ACIM, in contrast to other spiritual books, should not be "interpreted" symbolically at all. ACIM shall be taken in a very literal way, else the ego will make something entirely different out of it.

Inspired by Jesus' description of Himself as "The Way", I decided to title my book "Stairway to Heaven", and decided that the goal of the book was to inspire the reader to accept ACIM as a literal instruction for finding this Stairway and for how to climb it, one step at a time.

Stairway   Lars Gimstedt

May 22, 2347. NSA Report.

****

```
NSA Report 2346-1001-4240
TOP SECRET. CLF code 0.
Department for The Transhuman Threat.
May 22 2347.
Unmonitored disappearances.
Case study TTT-JZ-1.
```

****

```
JZ has continued at an accelerated rate to
show up at different Stairway Centers, which
have increased their membership numbers in
an alarming rate.

The TSS disconnects, that now occur daily in
numerous places around the Earth, are
starting to cause severe system disturbances
that despite large efforts from the
technical support departments, have now and
then resulted in temporary close-downs of
the whole TSS system.

We also have to admit that our employee
personality screening has to be investigated
and improved, as there have been seven cases
of defected NSA-TTT agents. In all these
cases they have been stationed near a
Stairway Center, in order to infiltrate by
becoming members. So far no infiltration has
been successful, and interrogation of the
defected agents have not given any
```

information on how the Stairway people have managed to brainwash our agents, or how it has been possible to persuade them to defect. As far as we know, there has been no financial transfers in connection with this. One of these defected agents has even succeeded in causing a TSS interrupt, but he has been unwilling to disclose how he did it.

There are still no reports of any political activities initiated by the centers, except an increase in co-operation with environmental protection groups and vegetarian groups.

The disturbed TSS functionality although has made many countries to proclaim temporary war laws, which has initiated some degree of civil unrest.

There are some reports from our field agents of unexplained spontaneous recovery from fatal illness in Stairway members. Two cases of pancreas cancer, and one case of brain tumor. Preliminary medical examination by body scan made by TTT medical staff has revealed a seemingly complete remission. There has been earlier documented cases of brain tumor remission using PsychoNeuroImmunology (PNI), but no reports regarding spontaneous remission of pancreatic cancer have been found.

This might be still another, before not observed, effect of BQRF. The BQRF research has now been expanded to include the NSA-TTT medical departments as well.

Published theories from the Stairway movement indicate this, saying that the thought patterns for transformed perception will affect the body, although they claim that one can only heal oneself, not others. This resembles the theory of spontaneous healing of the PNI school of thought.

****

End of NSA Report 2346-1001-4240
TOP SECRET. CLF code 0.
May 22 2347.

****

Stairway   Lars Gimstedt

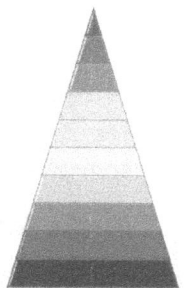

May 30, 2347.
Stairway New Zealand News.

Dear Sisters and Brothers

Our Center has grown tremendously over the last six months, and issuing this newsletter has become quite a large project. Several of you have taken on the task of assembling ten more photo-copiers, and distributing newsletters. I feel so grateful for this, without your help this task would have been impossible.

~.~. * .~.~

John's reminder of the importance of reading the Textbook, and not only do the exercises with the help of the lessons, felt important. I know I need to be reminded, as I like many of you automatically get

Stairway   Lars Gimstedt

"Today's Lesson" in the com, whilst reading the Textbook requires an active decision.

I have made the habit of scanning the Textbook each day for the "buzzwords" in the lesson of the day, to read the parts of the text that "happen to show up". I have found that this has deepened my understanding of the lessons. I have also found that by looking in the Text like this, I really understand the description of ACIM as being "holographic" – it is said somewhere in the text, that if you understand this part to 100%, you need not read further. Just like a hologram – each small part of it contains the whole, although maybe not in the same detail as a larger part.

This "holographic" method suits me, and might not suit everyone, but I would recommend every one of you to find your own way of consulting the Textbook regularly.

~.~. * .~.~

When reading how John worked through the stage he calls "Catching the Bull", I felt that this is the point I have arrived at, in my personal path. It feels both a

Stairway Lars Gimstedt

little depressing to have so far left to travel, but also comforting to hear Jesus assure

> "I do not believe that there is an order of difficulty in miracles; you do. I have called and you will answer. I understand that miracles are natural, because they are expressions of love. My calling you is as natural as your answer, and as inevitable." (T-4.IV.11)

It was very interesting to take part of John's psychological expertize in his description of the different levels of emotion. And also a good reminder of that the path to Awakening is not only a <u>mental</u> path. The inner change process has to include <u>all</u> parts of the illusion we perceive as "me" — my thoughts, my emotions and my body. I think that when ACIM talks about "thought process" we should interpret this as <u>everything</u> happening "inside": thoughts, intuitions, emotions, body reactions, moods, mental state, etc.

Reading John's description, I could recognize how I have not reached farther up on the "emotion scale" than "Trust". If feels good that I at least have a self-image saying "I am OK" (which if you remember me telling you, it wasn't when I was a teenager). But, I really long for the time when my self-image is characterized by "I want", knowing what I deep down really want in every situation, being inspired by my Self, and therefore truly creative.

But, at least I know what I want to do <u>now</u>, which is to work with information / teaching at our Center. Knowing, with what lesson 108 teaches me, that

> "To give and to receive are one in truth.
> I will receive what I am giving now."

Until next time, with love

Lena Adamson

~.~.~.~. * .~.~.~.~

Stairway   Lars Gimstedt

July 20, 2347.
BLOG ENTRY: Gentling the Bull – Beliefs.

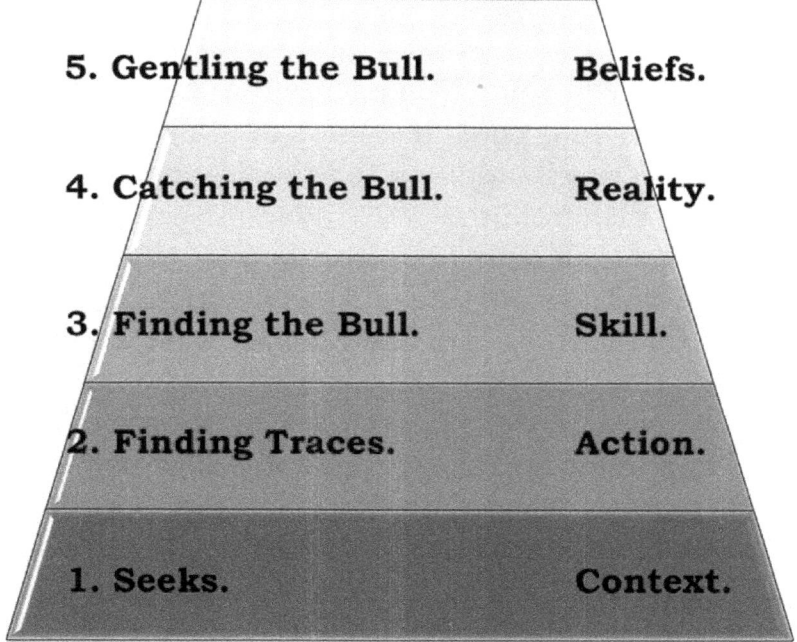

Welcome back to my blog! I can see in the traffic measurements that there now are almost half a billion followers. (No, this is not a typo – that is billion, not million!)

I have been interrogated by NSA about the cases of miraculous healing of Stairway members, and this time I sensed that the NSA agents really wanted to understand, instead of trying to find "evil" agendas behind things. I tried to explain to them that the body, being a neutral thing, just reacts to what the mind does. That this was something Jesus tried (in vain) to explain already 2300 years ago, when each time people witnessed a miraculous healing, He said to the healed person *"Your faith has healed you"* (Matthew 9:22, Mark 5:34, 10:52, Luke 8:48, 18:42). But, I do not think that these "old reports" impressed them...

There have been some NSA agents that have left their employments to become members at Stairway, and one of these has in addition to this disappeared a couple of times from the "TSS radar". Because of this, I have also had lengthy discussions with NSA about us "brainwashing" NSA agents. I have tried to explain to them that their agents had reached their decisions to quit working for NSA after having borrowed information material from us, after having studied these, and after having had long talks with us during several months. These former agents have been more than willing to talk with their former employer, but my feeling is that the interrogation people have just become more and more frustrated by their inability to understand why the defections have happened.

As with all people dominated by the ego's thought models of threat and scarcity, I think that many employed by authorities, or affiliated with conservative political groups, may start to feel threatened by the increasing interest of ACIM all over the world. There have been cases of open animosity, even violence, towards Stairway members, which luckily so far have resulted in not more than material damage. But, I want to urge you all: protect your right to think freely by verbal means, but do not counter-attack, not even verbally. Each time you surrender to these ego impulses, you will back up on your personal spiritual paths with many years, even hundreds of years. And every time you despite all "logic" forgive those who want to attack you, you will advance hundreds of years, maybe even thousands.

I cannot prove this, of course, but I ask you to open up into believing that this is the case:

> *The miracle substitutes for learning that might have taken thousands of years. It does so by the underlying recognition of perfect equality of giver and receiver on which the miracle rests. The miracle shortens time by collapsing it, thus eliminating certain intervals within it.*
> *(T-1.II.6)*

Acceptance and belief

And this brings us to the concept of Belief, the topic of today's blog entry. Last blog entry was about opening up oneself to the notion of a spiritual realm that is *not* "another part" of a larger reality, but a realm that *is* the only reality there is.

In 2020, when I had come a good way into compiling my book, I realized that this period, this effort, could be symbolized quite accurately by the fifth image of "The Bull and His Herdsman" – "Gentling the Bull" - under which it says

> *If but one thought arises, then another and another follows in an endless round.*
>
> *Through awakening, everything becomes truth; through delusion, it becomes error.*

Stairway Lars Gimstedt

Things do not come into being depending on circumstances but arise from the herdsman's own heart.

Hold the rein tight and do not allow any wavering.

I took warning from the first poem beneath the picture:

> *Not for a moment may the herdsman
> drop whip and rein.*
>
> *Or the bull would break free
> and stampede into the dust.*
>
> *But once patiently trained and made truly gentle,*
>
> *He follows the herdsman without halter or chain.*

But at the same time took comfort from the third one:

> *In patient training the bull got used to the herdsman and is truly gentle.*

Stairway

Lars Gimstedt

*Should he walk right into dust,
he now no longer gets dirty.*

*Long and patient gentling! In one sudden plunge
the herdsman has won his whole fortune.*

*Under the trees, others encounter his mighty
laugh.*

In the terms of my "Levels of emotion" image from my old e-course, I recognized that I had advanced to the level called "Acceptance". I was now not only open to and *willing* to see reality differently, I was starting to *accept* the fact that the physical world is not part of Truth and I had started to open up into truly *believing* it.

I found it thought-provoking that this level described the primary emotional state as Forgiveness, the corresponding thought process as Transcendent. And that the image of God now shows Compassion. Not compassion for our pleading for His forgiveness for our sinfulness, but for the fact that we have harbored such strange thoughts, those so often repeated in the Bible and other religious books – we are born sinful, we are worthless, and we can only be redeemed by sacrifice.

Rather, here compassion stands for an emotion similar to what the loving parent feels, watching his or her child having a terrible nightmare, and knowing that it is important to wake the child up gently, lest it gets trapped in the nightmare even after waking up.

Level	Emotion	Thought proc.	Self-image	Image of God
ILLUMINATION	(Indescribable)	Presence	I Am	I Am
PEACE	Bliss	Enlightenment	I am perfect	In everything
HAPPINESS	Joy	Transformation	I am whole	Embracing
LOVE	Love	Revelation	I am kind	Loving
REASON	Empathy	Abstraction	I am needed	Wise
ACCEPTANCE	**Forgiveness**	**Transcendence**	**I am human**	**Compassionate**
WILL	Optimism	Creation	I want	Inspiring
NEUTRALITY	Trust	Tolerance	I am OK	Creative
COURAGE	Firmness	Observance	I am growing	Allowing

In my e-course "A PS Perspective on ACIM" I had many years earlier inserted the image and the poems about "Gentling the Bull" at Lesson 121, so now I meditated on this lesson, and on some more lessons that I felt were connected with the Lesson 121:

Lesson 121. Forgiveness is the key to happiness.

Lesson 126. All that I give is given to myself.

Lesson 129. Beyond this world there is a world I want.

Lesson 130. It is impossible to see two worlds.

To keep believing

I now felt that my studies of ACIM during 35 years, and my psychological training and work experience, had started to give concrete and permanent results: I harbored a sense of inner peace almost all the time. When or if I became "caught off guard" and reverted to ego impulses, I always managed to stop myself, reconnect with my inner peace and ask for guidance from the Holy Spirit, and then act from the tranquil state of mind that inevitably was the result of this.

In ACIM chapter 6 "The Lessons of Love", in section V, "The Lessons of The Holy Spirit", it describes the three steps

> A. To Have, Give All to All.
> B. To Have Peace, Teach Peace to Learn It.
> C. Be Vigilant Only for God and His Kingdom.

And when reading ACIM's explanation of the third lesson, I understood that just believing in the *existence* of Truth is not enough. Constant vigilance against the ego was still necessary:

> This is a major step toward fundamental change. Yet it still has an aspect of thought reversal, since it implies that there is something you must be vigilant against.
>
> It has advanced far from the first lesson, which is merely the beginning of the thought reversal, and also from the second, which is essentially the identification of what is more desirable. This step, which follows from the second as the second follows from the first, emphasizes the dichotomy between the desirable and the undesirable. It therefore makes the ultimate choice inevitable.
>
> While the first step seems to increase conflict and the second may still entail conflict to some extent, this step calls for consistent vigilance against it. I have already told you that you can be as vigilant against the ego as for it. This lesson teaches not

only that you can be, but that you <u>must</u> be. It does not concern itself with order of difficulty, but with clear-cut priority for vigilance. This lesson is unequivocal in that it teaches there must be no exceptions, although it does not deny that the temptation to make exceptions will occur.

Here, then, your consistency is called on despite chaos. Yet chaos and consistency cannot coexist for long, since they are mutually exclusive. As long as you must be vigilant against anything, however, you are not recognizing this mutual exclusiveness, and still believe that you can choose either one. By teaching what to choose, the Holy Spirit will ultimately teach you that you need not choose at all. This will finally liberate your mind from choice, and direct it towards creation within the Kingdom.

This passage made me realize, that "territory won" by persistent strife, can be taken back in any moment. Realizing that even if I had come a long way, the fact remained – "I am only human", and sufficiently harsh circumstances could very probably make me revert into identifying with the ego completely again.

In hindsight, I see this period of my spiritual path as the most difficult up to this point in time, 2020, despite that many of the previous periods of my spiritual path had been turbulent, confusing, and full of interpersonal conflicts. I felt that I had accomplished so much with myself, with taking conscious control of my mind. But I also felt, more than before, the stealthy threats from my ego.

Stairway   Lars Gimstedt

Maybe because of the fact that I isolated myself from people whilst finalizing my book, I felt lonelier and more vulnerable than ever before. I had gained so much, and the mere thought of losing it again was terrifying.

But I also took comfort in reading Jesus reassurance:

> *Whenever fear intrudes anywhere along the road to peace, it is because the ego has attempted to join the journey with us and cannot do so.*
>
> *Sensing defeat and angered by it, the ego regards itself as rejected and becomes retaliative.*
>
> *You are invulnerable to its retaliation because I am with you. On this journey you have chosen me as your companion <u>instead</u> of the ego. Do not attempt to hold on to both, or you will try to go in different directions and will lose the way.*
>
> *(T-8.V.5)*

Stairway to Heaven

I published the book "Stairway to Heaven" in December 2021. It was soon sold in millions of copies, and I got many invitations to hold seminars about the book and about ACIM, and I was asked more and more often, the more known the book became.

My rather lonely and isolated life as a writer for three years had suddenly been switched over to the life of a busy lecturer.

Stairway — Lars Gimstedt

Many of the old ACIM discussion groups, that had used my e-course "A Psychosynthesis Perspective on ACIM" now started to use "Stairway to heaven" as their companion to ACIM, and many of the groups started to call themselves "The Stairway Movement".

This caught on, and soon almost all of the groups had adopted this name, and new groups with this name were formed, all over the world.

Again I felt the infinite importance of the "command" ACIM is giving us – *"Be Vigilant Only for God and His Kingdom."* – all this attention, all the media coverage, all the "important" people I got to meet, everything I experienced during this period of my life boosted my ego. I often had to remind myself of the line under the fifth Bull image – *"Not for a moment may the herdsman drop whip and rein."*

The Stairway Movement

Luckily, I did not fall for the temptation to build up a personal fortune from the revenues my book produced. With the help from some very skilled lawyers and finance experts from some of my first ACIM groups, we established a non-profit foundation, which we named "The Stairway Movement", as a tribute to all ACIM discussion groups of the world that had taken this name. Before we decided formally on the name, we conferred with every one of the groups, and we got unanimous acceptance.

I transferred all my money to the foundation, and we arranged so that I could be just an employee, with a reasonable salary. Two of my co-founders, more

Stairway

skilled than myself in organizing and managing, became the director and the finance manager. Later on, when the organization grew, more departments and managers were added. I took the role "Senior Adviser", a role I have retained all through the years with Stairway.

I could after this arrange all public speaking based on this foundation, which gave me full freedom to choose when and where to arrange seminars, courses, meetings, etcetera.

Among all "important" people I met, one meeting was especially gratifying. I met 2025 with Tenzin Gyatso, the 14:th Dalai Lhama, in Dharamsala, India. He was now 90 years old, but in good health. I was not much younger, 79, but I had admired him most of my life and he felt like a father to me.

True humility

I am so thankful to him, because getting to meet him was one of those things that really gave me a massive ego boost. I brought this problem up with him, and he laughed in his contagious way, and said *"Look at me! I am just a simple monk. So look at yourself – who are you?"* And thanks to this, I could remember who I really wanted to be – Senior Adviser - and what my Mission was.

When I came back to my hotel in Lhasa in the evening, I opened ACIM's Workbook in a random way, and Lesson 61 came up,
"I am the light of the world" and it reminded me of what ACIM means by humility:

Who is the light of the world except God's Son? This, then, is merely a statement of the truth about yourself. It is the opposite of a statement of pride, of arrogance, or of self-deception. It does not describe the self-concept you have made. It does not refer to any of the characteristics with which you have endowed your idols. It refers to you as you were created by God. It simply states the truth.

To the ego, today's idea is the epitome of self-glorification. But the ego does not understand humility, mistaking it for self-debasement.

Humility consists of accepting your role in salvation and in taking no other.

It is not humility to insist you cannot be the light of the world if that is the function God assigned to you. It is only arrogance that would assert this function cannot be for you, and arrogance is always of the ego.

True humility requires that you accept today's idea because it is God's Voice which tells you it is true. This is a beginning step in accepting your real function on earth. It is a giant stride toward taking your rightful place in salvation. It is a positive assertion of your right to be saved, and an acknowledgment of the power that is given you to save others.

In my next blog entry I will describe the next big step on my Path, which I took 2030. I moved to Iceland,

Stairway — Lars Gimstedt

where The Stairway Movement had started to build up its new main center.

The years up to this, from 2021 to 2029, had been the most hectic but also the most gratifying in my life. I felt secure in feeling that I always got, and most of the time was able to listen to, inner guidance from The Holy Spirit. I learned from the mistakes I made, that these were without exception the results of not listening inwards.

And, I also learned that listening inwards in a conscious, active and disciplined way, setting aside one hour each morning and one hour each evening for meditation, invariably led to decisions and actions that led me forwards on my Path. This positive feedback reinforced my belief in the existence of Truth, as opposed to the "truths" of the world.

Stairway   Lars Gimstedt

July 24, 2347. NSA Report.

```
***************************
NSA Report 2346-1001-4296
TOP SECRET. CLF code 0.
Department for The Transhuman Threat.
July 24 2347.
Unmonitored disappearances.
Case study TTT-JZ-1.
***************************
```

The rapid growth of The Stairway Movement, and the media coverage of this, has started to cause reactions, both from non-political as well as from political groups. These reactions have been positive and negative. The latter ones have often been expressed as fear of hidden agendas from the Stairway people, or fear of lobby pressure on political institutions. These suspicions have been reinforced by the fact that many of the world leaders have had meetings with JZ in Stairways headquarters on Iceland.

Civil unrest has occurred in many places, and in a riot in Madurai, India, the first case of killing a Stairway member has occurred. Seven persons were arrested for the fatal beating, but the legal system has got into juridical problems, as the dead body disappeared from the morgue during the night, and the victim reconnected to TSS after a couple of days in his home town, evidently unharmed.

Stairway

This invalidates our present plan for control via maser blast termination. The full implications of this resurrection have not yet been analyzed fully, but the security risk from penal activities rendered ineffective should not be underrated. NSA-TTT has accelerated the research on methods for isolating disturbing elements, but so far we do not have even a workable hypothesis on how to do this, when even death is no guarantee for isolation and control.

The internal security of NSA-TTT is also under close investigation and upgrade, after another five agents have defected.

We have tried to solve the disturbances of the TSS from disconnects and re-connects, which have caused more and more system breakdowns, sometimes for several days. Computing resources have been increased by 25%, and we have increased the number of surveillance probes with 50%. Strangely enough this has had no effect whatsoever, and we are presently investigating whether some kind of insider sabotage might be causing the problems.

In addition to this, the first cases of disconnects, where a re-connect has not happened at all have been documented, by visual observation from field agents, affirming the physical existence of the subjects involved.

Stairway Lars Gimstedt

This points at a disturbing fact that may threaten TSS in a fundamental way: the individuals failing to trigger TSS probes might have altered their RPNE (Remote Positron Neurologic Emission), which would necessitate a complete redesign of the TSS system.

We have ongoing contacts with all the defected agents. They have been forthcoming, seemingly having non-aggressive intentions regarding their defections, but discussions with them about the probe problems have not produced any usable data.

We have started to be restrictive about how to contact the defected agents, as they seem to have a stronger BQRF influence on our agents compared to other Stairway members, and we are now restricting contacts to be made by only our most senior agents. We also as a standard procedure now brain-scan our agents after they have returned to our base stations. We are hoping that this might reveal something about the defections, but so far we have got no relevant discrepancy data from these brain-scans.

****
End of NSA Report 2346-1001-4296
TOP SECRET. CLF code 0.
July 24 2347.
****

Stairway   Lars Gimstedt

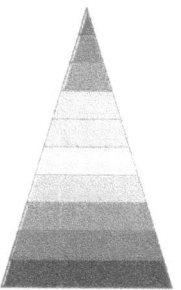

July 30, 2347.
Stairway New Zealand News.

Dear Sisters and Brothers

Now you are surely wondering why we now suddenly dare to send you this newsletter on your com, instead of getting it on paper from one of our messengers. Especially now, after our security is in question, with the killing in India (but as you know, it ended well). But, here is the fantastic explanation:

A couple of days ago Petur Bjarnason called me on my com. He is Information Manager at the Reykjavik Center, as you know, and he is my usual contact there. He asked me to go to our VR conference room. I assumed he wanted to have one of our usual VR meetings, and called our technician to meet me there so we could initiate the holographic projector in the chair we usually use for Petur.

Stairway Lars Gimstedt

To our initial shock, and then pleasant surprise, Petur already sat in his chair when we entered the conference room. He rose when I entered, and came up to me and gave me a hug, so I understood he was really there in the flesh. Shortly after, our security computer picked up his unannounced presence, and I had to tell the computer to clear him, explaining to the computer that he had come by space-time jump.

Despite that the ability for space-time-transit has developed over the last two hundred years, there is none on New Zealand that can do it, and I had never met anyone with this ability. So, after the initial surprise, I was really thrilled, and started to ask Petur about it. He understood my curiosity, but asked if it would not be better if he could tell us all at the Center about it. He said that he could stay a couple of days.

Together, we walked around the center, where I presented Petur to those that had not met him previously by VR conference, and we planned a seminar to take place the day after.

At the seminar, Petur led us through the techniques of the special form of meditation, body focus, and visualization needed to come into the state of mind where space-jump is possible. He told us that these were just prerequisites, a thorough understanding of Forgiveness and a thorough knowledge of ACIM's message is the base of the ability.

Petur got many questions, and one of them was whether space-jump ability could be misused. His answer was that the ability required such a deep understanding of the Course, and such a deep acceptance and devotion to the Atonement, that the probability is low, so low that to his knowledge (and one at the Main Center should know) it has never happened that the ability has been used for any other purpose than for Love. He quoted ACIMs lesson 46:

> "Those who forgive are thus releasing themselves from illusions, while those who withhold forgiveness are binding themselves to them."

Petur's answer didn't make us much wiser, but it felt reassuring.

After having listened to Petur's teaching at the seminar, we have all been practicing hard, as yet no one has made any breakthroughs. But, we are really working on it...

Stairway   Lars Gimstedt

Next monthly meeting we will hold a special workshop on this topic, so sign up for this, if you want to participate.

But, you are probably still wondering about why this newsletter comes on your com: Petur had two other purposes for his visit. One was to give us a new com crypto device, developed at the Main Center, which he said is designed on the base of the quantum twin theory. In the crypto software, we can specify all the receiving addresses, and the information self-destructs if it becomes diverted or intercepted. So now my work as the Information Manager will be a lot easier. I have come to like writing this newsletter by hand, so I will continue to use one of the old photocopiers, one which has a network connection.

Petur also had one more purpose with his visit here: it was to inform us that John Z is in the process of visiting all Stairway Centers all over the world, and that he has planned to visit us August 15, in connection to our next monthly meeting. I have never met him in person, so I am really thrilled! As I wrote you in March, I have met him via VR conference, but still, to meet him in person...

Stairway   Lars Gimstedt

~.~. * .~.~

Now to John's blog:

It was intriguing to read about NSA defections, as we at the Auckland Center have recently got two members that are former NSA agents. We had heard rumors about that this had happened elsewhere, but we didn't know for sure.

After their defection, these two men have been hassled a lot by NSA, and if it wasn't for TSS tracking, we would have offered to hide them in our homes. As it is now, we support them by always having one of us accompanying each one of them, so that they at least cannot be arrested with some invented charge.

They have provided us with useful information on how TSS works, and information on the organization we have heard about but have had very little information on, NSA-TTT, The "Department for The Transhuman Threat". Useful and chilling information...

~.~. * .~.~

Stairway — Lars Gimstedt

NSA has obviously also started to take an interest in "miraculous healing", which is something that we have discussed a lot at our meetings, and which also is a subject that arouses a lot of strong emotions.

I think it is important, in connection to health and sickness, to remind oneself of what ACIM says.

Firstly, how to look at sickness:

> "Perceive in sickness but another call for love, and offer your brother what he believes he cannot offer himself. Whatever the sickness, there is but one remedy.
> You will be made whole as you make whole, for to perceive in sickness the appeal for health is to recognize in hatred the call for love. And to give a brother what he really wants is to offer it unto yourself, for your Father wills you to know your brother as yourself.
> Answer his call for love, and yours is answered. Healing is the Love of Christ for His Father and for Himself."
> (T-12.II.3)

Secondly, that miracles heal the mind, not the body:

> "The miracle returns the cause of fear to you who made it. But it also shows that, having no effects, it is not cause, because the function of causation is to have effects.
> And where effects are gone, there is no cause. Thus is the body healed by miracles because they show <u>the mind made sickness, and employed the body to be victim</u>, or effect, of what it made."
> (T-28.II.11)

Thirdly, that the <u>purpose</u> of healing is to Awaken, not to reinforce the identification with the body:

> "The use of miracles as spectacles to induce belief is a misunderstanding of their purpose."
> (The tenth Miracle Principle, T-1.I.10.)

Next newsletter will be about John's visit here, so tag this stream to give you an alert!

Until next time, with love

Lena Adamson

Stairway Lars Gimstedt

~.~.~.~. * .~.~.~.~

Stairway   Lars Gimstedt

September 19, 2347.
BLOG ENTRY: Returning Home – Values.

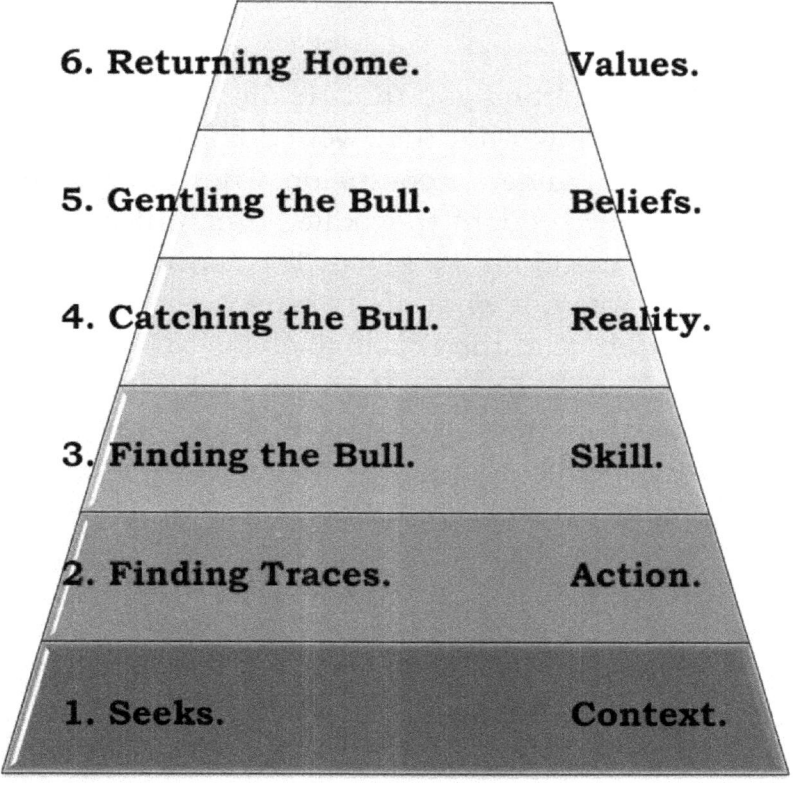

Welcome back! Today would have been my 401:th birthday, if time was linear. As it is not (it doesn't exist at all, but you may not believe this yet), it is more like my 101:th.

***

First, I want to comment on the killing of a Stairway member in the riot in India. As you surely know, all went well as he restored himself to his home town, and we have really managed to confuse the NSA. But, I also want to remind you all, as incidents like this lead to strong emotions, about what Jesus said already 2300 years ago: *"Forgive them, for they know not what they do."*

And I want to remind you that He did not mean that they did not know what they were doing because of their agitation, anger or confusion. They did *actually* not know: they thought they killed him, but had no idea that he could not be killed. The central message from Jesus was not what afterwards was proclaimed by the church, that the crucifixion was to be seen as God's sacrifice of His Only Begotten Son in order to atone for mankind's sins. Jesus' message was not about the crucifixion at all – it was about the resurrection:

> *"I am the resurrection and the life. Whoever believes in me, though he die, yet shall he live, and everyone who lives and believes in me shall never die."*
> (John 11:25)

And with "believe" he meant not believing that he had unique powers, but to just believe that death does not exist, not for him, and not for anyone else.

***

Many have commented on the fact that I have undergone rejuvenation treatment since I returned a year ago, criticizing us at the Center to not adhere to ACIMs view on sickness and aging.

Stairway Lars Gimstedt

I want to take the opportunity to respond to this criticism here.

First, let me quote ACIM, when Jesus talks about the fifty Miracle Principles:

> T-1.I.10. *The use of miracles as spectacles to induce belief is a misunderstanding of their purpose.*

I consulted my Inner Guide before taking a decision whether to accept medical treatment for my aging problems, and got the answer that it does really matter what I do in this world, and if I use things in this world as learning tools for The Holy Spirit, it can help me forward towards True Perception. If I on the other hand let my ego guide me, I will continue to be trapped, and I will attack others as well as myself.

As I have taken on the Mission of being "a Senior Adviser" to the ones that have been selected to be my pupils, my inner Teacher seems to say that whatever I can use to help me in this mission is OK.

So, as a general advice, I would like to quote ACIM again:

> *In any situation in which you are uncertain, the first thing to consider, very simply, is*
>
> *"What do I want to come of this? What is it for?"*
>
> *The clarification of the goal belongs at the beginning, for it is this which will determine the outcome.*
> *(T-17.VI.2.)*

Stairway Lars Gimstedt

This is not only something concerning what to believe.

It concerns core values:
What do I value the most?
What is it I consider to be holy for me?

And also, on a very practical, concrete, level: I intend to visit all the Stairway Centers of the world, and I need to stay healthy and strong to be able to fulfil this plan. Since my last blog entry I have visited another six Centers, visits that have felt rewarding, not only for the members I have visited, but for myself. This really reminds me of what the Course says about giving (from Lesson 159):

> *To give is how to recognize you have received.*
> *It is the proof that what you have is yours.*

***

With this in parts negative prelude of this blog entry, some good news:

The number of active Stairway Movement members has now reached one billion!

Some claim that it has been the most fast-growing religion ever, but I think it is wise to remind oneself about what ACIM says about this:

> *The curriculum the Course proposes is carefully conceived and is explained, step by step, at both the theoretical and practical levels. It emphasizes*

> *application rather than theory, and experience rather than theology.*
>
> *It specifically states that "a universal theology is impossible, but a universal experience is not only possible but necessary" (Manual, p. 77).*
>
> *Although Christian in statement, the Course deals with universal spiritual themes. It emphasizes that it is but one version of the universal curriculum.*
>
> *There are many others, this one differing from them only in form. They all lead to God in the end.*
>
> *(Preface / What it is.)*

Jesus never meant to create a new religion, not year 35, neither year 1976, not now. I think one is wise not regarding ACIM students as belonging to a new religion, rather they are people united in their own individual inner processes of finding their Selves, with the ultimate goal of waking up to *"an universal experience"* of One-ness with each other and with God.

We are united in our <u>core values</u>, where we are waking up into realizing that the physical universe lacks intrinsic meaning and therefore has no real value, and realizing that what we are finding <u>has</u> value is Truth, which will help us find our True Identity.

✶✶✶

Iceland

This brings me back to the telling of the story about my path, where the next period of my life can be characterized by the expression "Returning home to my core values."

The location of the main Stairway Center in Seattle, USA, was experienced by many of us as not optimal. NSA-TTT constituted an increasing disturbance, taking more and more of our valuable time that we really wanted to spend teaching. Members in other nations voiced their concern about the integrity of The Stairway Movement and the risk for infiltration. We were not afraid of this ourselves, but the concern of our members took away focus from our real mission.

The idea came up at the Center about relocating to a more neutral place, and we started up a project, in which an inventory of all plausible locations was made. We found thousands of viable, some even perfect, places, but in the end the choice fell on Iceland.

I cannot go into everything that led to this decision, but I can mention a few contributing factors.

Our impression of the Icelandic people was that they were open-minded, but at the same time not gullible. In the Icelandic strongly egalitarian culture, leaders of all kind were viewed with caution. On Iceland there is no fertile ground for gurus or self-proclaimed experts. Iceland had legal systems well suited to our needs for communicating with the world. The technological level was extremely high, and could well support our needs for developing and maintaining our technical systems. Iceland had kept outside all international organizations and treaties, keeping with their more than one thousand year old tradition of being a culturally, economically and politically independent people.

So during the period 2030 to 2035, the Center moved to new premises on the small island Videy, just north of central Reykjavik. The country of Iceland gave us a large piece of land just west of the Imagine Peace Tower (initiated and designed by the artist Yoko Ono 2007). We built our new Center below the monument, near the shore, with a magnificent view over the ocean, with central Reykjavik to the left and the glacier Snaefelljökull on the other side of a vast bay, where one could see the snowy peaks rise above the horizon to the right.

Stairway — Lars Gimstedt

I moved there with my wife Hi'ilani. Mine and Hi'ilani's children were not children any longer, all my children were now all grownups, the younger ones were 30 and 32, the elder ones 49 and 52, and they were all well established in the Seattle area, and wanted to stayed there.

Our living quarters were inside the Center, where I and Hi'ilani had a small apartment, although with a couple of guest rooms, on the second floor in one of the four wings of the central office building. The others in the Stairway management group, which now has grown to five persons, had similar apartments in the other wings. When we moved in, the others had already moved into the center with their families.

Already used to the varyingly sunny and rainy weather of Seattle, we could adjust rather well to the Icelandic climate, where the temperature was never really high, but also never really low, due to the warm Gulf Stream that flows northward just west of Iceland.

Returning home

Now began a period of my life, that I in hindsight can call "Returning home". Not home to Iceland, which I actually had only visited briefly before, but home to my core values. When we had come past the rather chaotic period of resettling to a new country and a new culture, I felt that my sense of inner peace was becoming reinforced. Partly due to the fact that I was now living inside a Stairway Center, but very much due to the "harmonious vibrations" of the nature around us, the silence, the clean air.

I had searched, I had found the first traces, I had found my real Self, I had managed to "catch" my thought patterns, I had persistently learnt to control them, and now I was returning home to my True Self.

In my daily morning and evening meditations, I returned again to my old image of Levels of Emotions, and it felt like I had reached the level Reason: The reason I was here was to better pursue my mission. The reason for my mission was to teach empathy. Doing this *required my ability for reason*, for clear thinking. My self-image had passed the false humility of the ego, which is really self-debasement, to become the honest statement "I am needed", together will all other "teachers" and Miracle Workers.

Level	Emotion	Thought proc.	Self-image	Image of God
ILLUMINATION	(Indescribable)	Presence	I Am	I Am
PEACE	Bliss	Enlightenment	I am perfect	In everything
HAPPINESS	Joy	Transformation	I am whole	Embracing
LOVE	Love	Revelation	I am kind	Loving
REASON	**Empathy**	**Abstraction**	**I am needed**	**Wise**
ACCEPTANCE	Forgiveness	Transcendence	I am human	Compassionate
WILL	Optimism	Creation	I want	Inspiring
NEUTRALITY	Trust	Tolerance	I am OK	Creative
COURAGE	Firmness	Observance	I am growing	Allowing

Distraction versus abstraction

The image of the levels of emotions describes the dominant thought process at this level as "abstraction" which I first found a bit confusing, until I meditated on the sixth image of "The Bull and His Herdsman" – "Returning Home on the Back of the Bull":

Stairway Lars Gimstedt

Now the struggle is over!
Gain and loss, too, have fallen away.

The herdsman sings an old folk song or plays a nursery tune on his flute. Looking up into the blue sky, he rides along on the back of the bull.

If someone calls after him, he does not look back; nor will he stop if tugged by the sleeve.

"Abstraction" meant for me that I was now no longer <u>di</u>stracted from My True Thoughts by everything happening around in the world. I could, despite the "concrete" disturbances from the outside, stay in my True Mind, which belongs to that which is formless, timeless, and therefore abstract in the truest sense:

> *God, Who encompasses all being, created beings who have everything individually, but who want to share it to increase their joy.*
>
> *Nothing real can be increased except by sharing. That is why God created you.*

> *Divine Abstraction* takes joy in sharing. That is what creation means. "How," "what" and "to whom" are irrelevant, because real creation gives everything, since it can create only like itself.
>
> Remember that in the Kingdom there is no difference between having and being, as there is in existence. In the state of being the mind gives everything always.
>
> (T-4.VII.5)

Lesson 161 also emphasizes this:

> *Complete abstraction* is the natural condition of the mind. But part of it is now unnatural. It does not look on everything as one. It sees instead but fragments of the whole, for only thus could it invent the partial world you see.
>
> The purpose of all seeing is to show you what you wish to see. All hearing but brings to your mind the sounds it wants to hear.

And in my meditations on the theme Returning Home, I found these lessons to be good reminders of what my task was now:

> *Lesson 151. All things are echoes of the Voice for God.*
>
> *Lesson 155. I will step back and let Him lead the way.*

Thy will be done

This expression from the Lord's Prayer has often been misunderstood, as giving up what one wants and surrendering to someone else's will, in this case God's.

The common interpretation has been that we are "*Weak and sinful, poor and blind*", and therefore unworthy of getting our own will through. The only correct part of this expression is the word "blind", the rest is the ego's postulates, in trying to get us to believe in salvation through sacrifice.

ACIM gives a new meaning to "Thy will be done":

When I awaken into knowing who I really am, One with God, I will discover that what I want most of all, what I value most of all, is to let God's Will be done. Then there is no sacrifice; then there is none of the ego's false humility, which is mere debasement.

During these years, I felt more and more "at home" in letting go of my ego impulses, listening inwards and hearing the Voice of God as new impulses, new thoughts, new ideas, which all had one thing in common – love and compassion, all the time forgiving my brothers and sisters for their "sins".

I still experienced ego impulses, sometimes even strongly, but I had with persistent practice now learnt to gracefully just let them be, without acting on them, until they subsided, and then do what I really wanted to do: *"Step back and let Him lead the way"*.

September 23, 2347. NSA Report.

```
*************************

NSA Report 2346-1001-4354
TOP SECRET. CLF code 0.
Department for The Transhuman Threat.
September 23 2347.
Unmonitored disappearances.
Case study TTT-JZ-1.

*************************

JZ has from September 19, when he turned 101
biologically, mostly stayed at the Center on
Iceland. He has here received many visits
from different groups, world leaders, and
high church representatives.

The massive increase of Stairway members has
got large media coverage, and most
governments and church officials are very
active in analyzing the potential impacts of
this on security and political control.

He has made one trip, to the Vatican, where
JZ attended a closed meeting with the Pope
and high officials. No information from this
meeting has been released. But there can be
no coincidence that the Catholic Church
after this meeting has announced it is
contemplating changes in its fundamental
theological postulates in controversial
areas like sexual affinity, Virgin Birth,
and others.
```

Stairway   Lars Gimstedt

The secret process behind China's and India's recent treaty has been analyzed by NSA-TTT. In this treaty, they closed down all territorial disputes, initiated new open trade regulation, and started a project for introducing a common currency for entire Asia as the first step towards a global currency.

We have acquired information of that the preparation work force for this treaty included a large number of persons closely affiliated with the Stairway Movement. This is the first time we have confirmed a definite political activity from them. Together with the rapidly decreasing efficacy of the TSS system on Stairway members, this constitutes a very substantial loss of NSA's abilities for political correction and population control.

To the dismay of the authors of this report, this has caused an internal controversy at NSA-TTT, which has been disruptive on prioritization and coordination of our efforts.

We are not free to disclose anything more than this, but we would welcome immediate decisions on NSA policies. This is an urgent need, especially as this internal problem is causing an increasing rate of agent defections to the Stairway Movement. We even have difficulties in assessing the risk for downright infiltration from Stairway.

Another blatant example of the rapidly increasing political influence from Stairway is the fact that the 18th Dalai Lhama just moved back to Lhasa, probably as an effect of secret agreements in the above mentioned treaty between China and India. In the restored palace in Lhasa, Dalai Lhama has now established a Buddhist Stairway Center! This center replaces the old Stairway Center that was located just nearby.

Radical changes of Buddhist postulates have been published, for example have they now proclaim Jesus as a possible incarnation of Buddha.

****

End of NSA Report 2346-1001-4354
TOP SECRET. CLF code 0.
September 23 2347.

****

Stairway   Lars Gimstedt

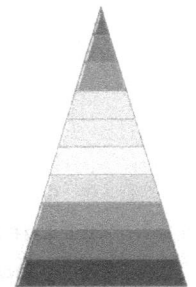

September 30, 2347.
Stairway New Zealand News.

Dear Sisters and Brothers

John's visit here August 15:th was a wonderful experience, and I know I am not speaking only for myself. After having experienced Petur Bjarnason's jump here, suddenly meeting John inside our premises wasn't the same "jump scare", especially as we had been forewarned about his arrival.

The monthly meeting had got extraordinarily many members to announce that they planned to participate, so we had to relocate to the Auckland sports stadium in order to accommodate all.

I had expected John to give some pre-prepared speech or lecture, and I was surprised when he asked us to prepare the meeting with a large number of mics that

Stairway — Lars Gimstedt

could be passed around in the audience. (We managed to get hold of two hundred mics!) At the meeting, he didn't use the stage except for his initial short welcoming speech — most of the time, three hours, he spent walking around answering questions from us in the auditorium, everybody connected to the PA system. Only at the end he returned to the stage, to lead a long visualization called The Evolution, which he wrote way back, 2013, for his first e-course about ACIM, "A Psychosynthesis Perspective on ACIM", that most of you may have heard about, but maybe not looked into.

As many of you participated in the meeting, or have talked to people that did, I will not try to recapitulate all the questions and answers during the meeting. But I still want to describe the quality of the meeting. With the authenticity from his answering the questions that were on people's minds, and then answering questions that followed from his answers, it was a learning experience that surpassed any pre-prepared lecture John could have done. It gave me so much, and I have got feed-back from many saying the same thing.

Stairway — Lars Gimstedt

With this, now to John's latest blog entry.

Stairway's move to Iceland is something we all learn about in school, but reading John's version of it made it feel more authentic, especially together with the description of where John was on his own Path during that period of Stairway's history. That the move there felt as "coming home" for him, despite the fact that he had only visited Iceland briefly before.

With "coming home" I think he primarily means coming home into realizing what is really important for oneself. Risking being a bit pompous I would even say, finding the true purpose of one's life.

John was 84 when he moved to Iceland, and I don't think he didn't know what the purpose of his life was until then. Rather, what I think he meant by "coming home" was he had now fully accepted the notion of what his Mission with capital M was; he had integrated it into his personality, and he really wanted to fulfil it whole-heartedly.

One might conclude that this is something that always will come late in one's life, but I don't think this must be the case. Firstly, I know of numerous examples of persons having reached this point much earlier in their lives. Secondly, we have to consider the fact that ACIM was at that time still quite unknown. Most of the population of Earth hadn't heard of ACIM. There was still numerous religious wars going on, fuelled by manipulative politicians and brainwashed fundamentalists, so as Jesus is quoted in Matthew 13:

> "A sower went out to sow. And as he sowed, some seeds fell along the path, and the birds came and devoured them. Other seeds fell on rocky ground, where they did not have much soil, and immediately they sprang up, since they had no depth of soil, but when the sun rose they were scorched. And since they had no root, they withered away. Other seeds fell among thorns, and the thorns grew up and choked them."

Today, people may be hard-headed and difficult to persuade to think in other ways they have been accustomed to do, but at least most people today adhere to logic and scientific stringency. ACIM is extremely logical, despite its radically different view on reality. ACIM does not dismiss the inherent logic of science, it only describes is as part of a very logical and convincing illusion. Therefore, the reaction in our time is mostly one of openness and interest, albeit watchful. The "re-thinking" displayed by our brothers the former NSA agents is a good example of this. As Matthew 13 ends:

> "Other seeds fell on good soil and produced grain, some a hundredfold, some sixty, some thirty. He who has ears, let him hear."

~.~. * .~.~

"Thy will be done"

This is an old Christian expression, which people in modern times have had difficulties with. In medieval times people were indoctrinated into blindly following the orders of authorities, where the Church was the dominant one. But, in the era of increasing individualism, the expression "Thy will be done" felt more and more like oppression, like the priests were asking us to sacrifice our personal freedom.

But, what John talks about in his blog, and which he also talked a lot about at our meeting, was that when meditating for example on Lesson 155 "I will step back and let Him lead the way", he felt that he had "come home" to the conviction this was _really_ what he wanted himself. So I think what John means is that the old expression "Thy will be done" now can be used as _an active and conscious decision_.

As the very last ACIM lessons says:

"He is in charge _by my request_."

Until next time, with love

Lena Adamson

~.~.~.~. * .~.~.~.~

November 16, 2347.
BLOG ENTRY: Bull Forgotten – Self-image.

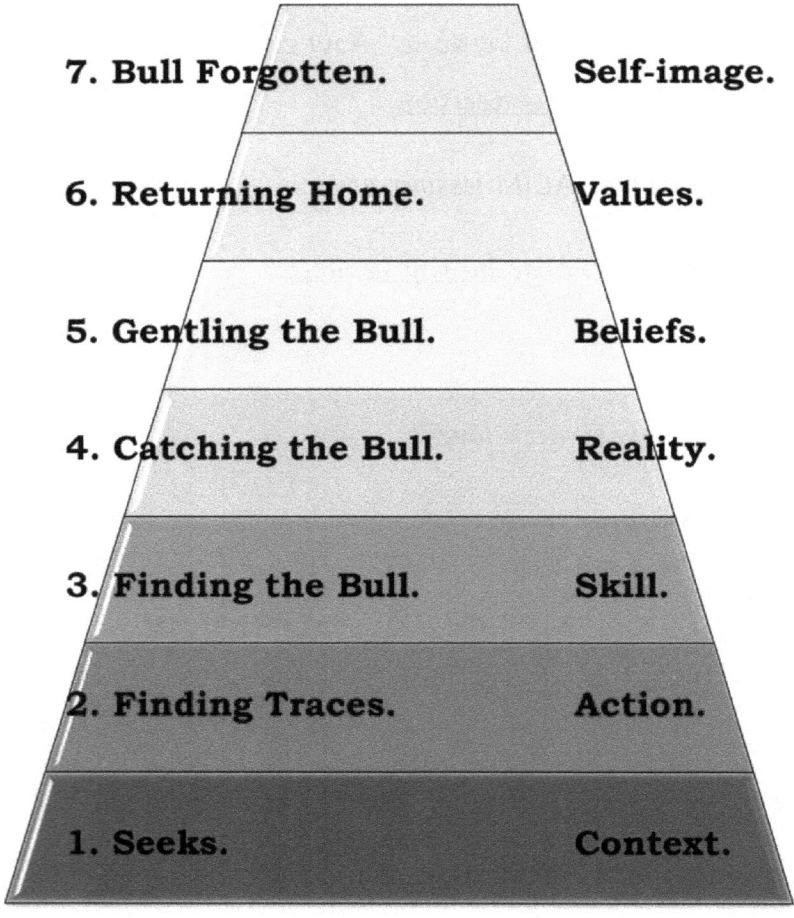

Welcome back.

This blog entry will start with very good news, which naturally is old news for all of you, but news that is worth repeating.

Stairway Lars Gimstedt

The new China-India treaty is the first definite sign of that the world is in a near future heading towards true world peace, for the first time in human history.

The new signals from the Catholic Church, and the establishing of the Buddhist Stairway Center in Lhasa are clear signs of an increasing unification of the world's religions.

One could raise the objection that the latter is happening due to the fact that the number of Stairway members has now reached 1,5 billion, but I personally want to believe that the nearing of different theological schools is the result of a global spiritual awakening.

The NSA surveillance has suddenly decreased, and I have had no meetings with them since my last blog entry. I do not know what the reason for this is, but I suspect that there can be a connection to the fact that an increasing number of old NSA agents have become new Stairway members. Many of these have indicated that NSA are suffering from internal problems.

We here at the Main Center do not really care what kind of problems they are having, but we hope that there might be some divine influence, pushing things there in a positive direction…

I suspect that NSA's underlying problem is about self-image. They have seen themselves as the sole protectors of world peace, and now when world peace is materializing without their co-operation, even despite their efforts to slow things down, they have become insecure: "If we no longer are the most important entity for protecting world peace, who are we?"

***

Self-Image

This brings me to the topic of this blog entry: Self-Image.

The period 2035 to 2040, when I was 89 to 94, was the most peaceful in my life until then. My state of mind had settled down into a constant meditative state, in which there was no more need for vigilance against ego impulses. Naturally, sometimes things happened that made me upset, feel sorrow, or anger, or some other negative emotion, but by my "spine reaction" of forgiving the ones involved completely, at once restored my sense of inner peace.

I was no longer identified with my thoughts and on the varying contents of my thought processes. My sense of identity was now firmly based on a self-image telling me: "I am one who has complete trust in The Holy Spirit as his reliable Inner Guide, and he has always access to his Inner Peace."

I found my old "mantra" from the period in 2013 when I was compiling the e-course about ACIM, and I now had that as a part of my daily meditation:

I am here only to be truly helpful.

I am here to represent Him Who sent me.

I do not have to worry about what to say or what to do, because He Who sent me will direct me.

(T2-V:A.18)

In these mediations, I also included the seventh image from "The Bull and His Herdsman", "Bull Forgotten – Man Remains", together with the text underneath:

There are not two Dharmas*. Provisionally only has the bull been set up, somewhat in the nature of a sign-post. He might also be likened to a snare for catching hares, or to a fishing net.

Now the herdsman feels as when the shining gold has been separated out from the ore, or as when the moon appears from behind a cloud bank.

> *The one cool light has been shining brilliantly since the time before the beginning.*
>
> *(* Dharmas= teachings)*

For me "Bull Forgotten" meant that I no longer needed to watch my thought processes at all. My professional training as a psychotherapist had made me use all kinds of models with which I could describe different kinds of thought processes. "Bull Forgotten" meant also that I could forget these models as well, in regard to my own thoughts.

This meant that my self-image had changed in a fundamental way. I had let go of an ancient cultural belief, promoted by the philosopher René Descartes, and which had dominated Western culture: *"I think, therefore I am."*

I truly felt a sense of my new, and truer, self-image when I meditated on the ACIM lessons 221 and 229:

> *Lesson 221. Peace to my mind.*
> *Let all my thoughts be still.*

> *Lesson 229. Love, which created me,*
> *is what I am.*

Like in mind, so on earth.

The inner state of my mind gracefully projected itself on my outer life.

I no longer traveled the world, except to participate in the inaugurations of new Imagine Peace Towers that were installed in each of the Stairway Centers. The project of doing this had started 2032, in co-operation with Yoko Ono. The first Tower was installed 2033 in the Center in Lhasa where it was at that time, on Yoko's 100th birthday. She lived to see another fifty Towers be installed, before she passed away 2039.

In Reykjavik, I met with visiting individuals and groups, often leading group meditations on different topics.

I took up my psychotherapeutic practice, in which I still used techniques and methods from Psychosynthesis, CBT and NLP, but where the focus now was on simultaneous personal *and* spiritual growth based on ACIM's text and lessons.

In my practice, I now adhered completely to ACIM's view on psychotherapy. In the introduction of the part "Psychotherapy. Purpose, Process and Practice" it says

> *Psychotherapy is a process that changes the view of the self. At best this "new" self is a more beneficent self-concept, but psychotherapy can hardly be expected to establish reality. That is not its function. If it can make way for reality, it has achieved its ultimate success.*
>
> *Its whole function, in the end, is to help the patient deal with one fundamental error; the belief that anger brings him something he really wants, and that by justifying attack he is protecting himself. To whatever extent he comes to realize that this is an error, to that extent is he truly*

saved.
(P-2.in.1.)

Jumping outside the illusion

In September 2040, I started to get what I then thought were optical disturbances caused by some infirmity of old age, in which I saw halos around objects and persons, and other light effects.

I first became a little concerned, but when our physician at the Centre had used both eye camera and brain scan and found nothing alarming, I relaxed. The only thing he commented on was that my brain scan revealed an unusually homogeneous pattern, a sign of complete tranquility and inner harmony.

These optical "disturbances" had been happening for a month, when I one day used a special visualization during my morning meditation. In this visualization, I imagined myself climbing up to the top of Videy, the island the Centre is located on. The reason for visualizing this, was that my old knees did not any longer permit me to climb up there as often as I wished, to look at the magnificent view from up there.

The long meditation before doing the visualization had probably put me in a state of deep hypnotic trance, resulting in that I experienced the visualization as exceptionally vivid, and I was really enjoying being up at the top of the mountain. I took in the full experience of it with all my senses simultaneously, feeling the ocean breeze against my face, smelling the scents of the ocean and of the fishing vessels out in the bay, experiencing all the pleasurable emotions aroused from standing here. I remember how the thought came up *"It is so real, despite being just a dream. It feels like being God, creating the world."*

And the thought interrupted my visualization, in somehow moving me from being a participant into observing my visualization as an observer outside myself, and the thought awoke me from my trance. To my utter surprise, I now found myself standing at the very mountain top I had been visualizing.

I first became frightened and confused, by the mere shock of this utter disruption of my sense of reality. Then, when my heart rate slowed down, I started to think about whether this could be a sudden attack of psychosis. But, I sat down on the grass, and tried to calm myself, and to think clearly. I looked at my watch, and discovered that the whole day had passed, and it was suddenly late afternoon.

I started to walk down the mountain trail, well-known to me from numerous walks here before. I arrived at the Center, where people I met just asked me if I had had a nice walk, and then they continued with their business.

Still shaken up, I consulted ACIM, to see whether Jesus has said anything about this kind of experience, but found nothing specific. But, when I happened to look at lesson 265, I felt some kind of inner resonance:

LESSON 265.

Creation's gentleness is all I see.

I have indeed misunderstood the world, because I laid my sins on it and saw them looking back at me. How fierce they seemed! And how deceived was I to think that what I feared was in the world, instead of in my mind alone.

Today I see the world in the celestial gentleness with which creation shines. There is no fear in it.

Let no appearance of my sins obscure the light of Heaven shining on the world. What is reflected there is in God's Mind. The images I see reflect my thoughts. Yet is my mind at one with God's. And so I can perceive creation's gentleness.

In the visualization, this was how I had decided to see the world. And I understood that it was *my decision* for doing this that was primarily involved in what had happened. Together, of course, with the state of my mind at the time, a state of complete peace and contentment, a deep trust that everything is completely OK.

Being real takes practice

I knew that what happened was the beginning of leaving the illusion of the physical world, and that it had happened involuntarily did not mean that it could not be repeated.

Stairway   Lars Gimstedt

Eagerly, I repeated the trance work and the visualization each day, careful with what I selected as "target", so I would not end up somewhere I could not come back from.

To my disappointment first, I could not repeat my "teleportation", but I realized that this must be a skill that could be modeled and practiced. So I persevered, changing the meditation technique and the visualizations in small steps.

After a couple of week's persistent daily experimenting, I finally succeeded in transporting myself, this time to the northwest head of Videy, and the time lap this time turned out to be two days later. I walked the two kilometers back to the Center, feeling really elated, but had to try to become more solemn when I now met with my agitated friends and a very anxious wife. They had been looking for me, in larger and larger groups, for two days, the second day and night together with the Icelandic police.

After another two month's practice I had refined my "technique". I am though reluctant to call it just a technique, as the process feels mostly intuitive and subconscious. But, never the less, I could now control not only where to go, but also which point in time I wanted to target for. Backing in time proved to be impossible, which was a relief, due to all philosophical implications such a possibility would lead to.

When I had come this far, I disclosed all that had happened with all my friends at the center, which of course made all of them start practicing. None ever succeeded though – it is difficult to explain with words an intuitive process like this – and many started to regard me as "the miracle man". I opposed this, as I was convinced that anyone could learn to do this, but many gave up trying.

(But, to my relief, the knowledge of how to do it grew after I left, and when I now came back after 300 years, I was glad to discover that the space-time-jump ability has spread to many.)

Disturbing the illusion

What we did not realize the first time, was that the space-time-jumps of mine could not pass unnoticed – the global surveillance system was of course bound to catch it, as some kind of disrupted contact from the surveillance probes we could not see but knew that they were everywhere.

But we did realize it, when agents from NSA started to visit the center, interrogating me and others. I did not make a secret of what had happened, and I tried to disclose everything I knew and had understood of it. But, I sensed that they were extremely suspicious, and that they thought that I was withholding crucial information. There was nothing I could do about this, other than to continue to reassure them, but when they left us they always seemed to be in a sullen mood.

We got to know from a friend in Reykjavik, that NSA established a surveillance office outside Reykjavik with several permanent agents, instead of just having a lone agent stationed on Iceland.

A step, but not the last one

I knew that my first space-time jumps meant that I had taken a large step towards awakening from the illusion of the physical world, but I also understood that more steps would be needed. What ACIM says about this felt reassuring, although also confusing and paradoxical:

> *I have said that the last step in the reawakening of knowledge is taken by God. This is true, but it is hard to explain in words because words are symbols, and nothing that is true need be explained.*
> *(T-7.I.6)*

From my esoteric studies, I had for a long time known that statements about Truth, made from the level of the mind, which belongs to the domain of non-truth, can at best be experienced as "meaningful paradoxes", and it felt that this was pointedly expressed by the third poem beneath the seventh Bull image:

> *The herdsman has returned home.*
> *Now home is everywhere.*
>
> *When both things and self are wholly forgotten, peace reigns all day long.*
>
> *Believe in the peak 'Entrance of the Deep Secret' -*
>
> *No man can settle down on this peak.*

Stairway Lars Gimstedt

It felt like I had reached a sense of who I really was. I had on a deep level transformed my self-image, realizing that I was a Self, pure Spirit, an extension of God.

But I also really felt like I had arrived to "The Entrance of the Deep Secret", and I could not figure out how now to continue my "journey without distance".

Stairway   Lars Gimstedt

November 20, 2347. NSA Report.

```
*************************

NSA Report 2346-1001-4419
TOP SECRET. CLF code 0.
Department for The Transhuman Threat.
November 20 2347.
Unmonitored disappearances.
Case study TTT-JZ-1.

*************************
```

In JZ's last blog entry, he discloses how he discovered his neuroportation ability, and tries to explain the mechanisms. But, either he still wants to keep this a secret, or he is actually open and honest, as the information on this is exactly the same as given to our agents 2040.

He has now demonstrated that neuroportation can be used for space travel, by visiting the Moon Base a couple of days ago, where he led an inauguration ritual for another Image Peace Tower, installed at the center of the Moon Base. As the light beam itself cannot be seen in vacuum, the "tower" is instead an extremely bright multicolor laser, slowly changing its color through the visible color spectrum. The beam is programmed to scan over the surface of Earth, in such a way so it can be seen at each Stairway Center a certain evening each month during ten minutes at a specific time, each time going from deep red through the whole spectrum to light purple. On other places outside the Center areas it can also be seen, but just during one minute. The light ray is sufficiently bright to be seen even in daylight.

Analysis has been initiated to assess if there are hidden messages coded into the beam, or if there are any other hidden functions. As yet, none have been found, and the laser beam installation seems to have some kind of symbolic function only.

All Imagine Peace Towers have gotten large media coverage, contributing to the rapidly increasing public interest in the Stairway Movement, but this last installation, and JZ's "space jump", has caused larger coverage that ever before.

The ability to travel space with neuroportation raises the issue of possible contact with other civilizations, which constitutes a new severe security problem. This could also explain where individuals could reside during the time lapses between disappearance and re-appearance. These time lapses are in most cases hours or days, but JZ has recently proven that the time lapse can be 300 years.

This is although speculative, as no other data supports this hypothesis. Continued surveillance will although also focus on looking for data connected to extraterrestrial intelligence.

Since last report, NSA-TTT has been reorganized, and the top management has been replaced completely, after the defection to Stairway by one of the top managers. We are still awaiting new directives on how to handle assessed security risks, with respect to maser termination, but we are unfortunately still rendered unable to act, due to the lack of clear instructions.

In addition to agent defection to Stairway, which has continued to increase, there have also been incidents if disobedience from agents, forming their own action groups.

One of these action groups used unauthorized maser termination on three Stairway members found inside NSA-TTT premises in Sweden, talking to NSA employees, but before they could assess the results of the termination, the bodies had disappeared. TSS after a while re-connected with the terminated Stairway persons at other locations, where our agents later found them alive and unharmed. Even if we immediately after the incident managed to put the insubordinate NSA-TTT agents in isolated confinement, the information about this incident unfortunately spread anyhow, and has had a very demoralizing effects on all NSA-TTT agents.

There seems now to be a total lack of efficient counter-measures that we can use against Stairway. Even if they claim to be working for world peace, their apparent invulnerability exposes the world to extreme danger. It is vital that NSA develops abilities that matches those Stairway seems to have reached, lest we lose control completely of world politics and over governmental institutions. Scientific investigation and research has to increase to a sufficiently high level to ensure this – if the apparent scientific laymen of Stairway have found this knowledge and these abilities, our skilled scientists should be able as well.

We although unfortunately also have to report, that in addition to the defections of NSA-TTT agents, there have now come several defections from NSA-TTT experts and research scientists.

****

End of NSA Report 2346-1001-4419
TOP SECRET. CLF code 0.
November 20 2347.

****

Stairway   Lars Gimstedt

November 30, 2347.
Stairway New Zealand News.

Dear Sisters and Brothers

The Moon Base Imagine Peace Tower feels like a concrete sign of the rapid growth of Stairway, a sign that we will see regularly. According to HQ Center, our allotted time will be **the third day each month**, at **9:00 PM**. The light will be visible for 10 minutes. So, our first time will be **now on Monday December 3**!

Here at the center we will have an outdoor meditation gathering, starting at 8:30 PM that day. Everyone is invited!

If the weather is too cold, we will be indoors at the conference center, where we can turn the skylight opacity down. If it is cloudy, we will use real time satellite images on our conference screens.

Stairway — Lars Gimstedt

John's "space jump" has really made the news. And it has even more strengthened our resolve in our practicing, even if we know that

> "There is no order of difficulty in miracles.
> One is not 'harder' or 'bigger' than another.
> They are all the same. All expressions of love are maximal."
> (Miracle Principle no 1.)

We have little information more than what media have reported about the killings of the three Stairway members in Sweden. We received a short com message saying that they are back at their home countries, and are getting help for the trauma they naturally experienced. It was a relief that they belonged to the group of members having long experience of space-time jumps, which probably was crucial for their subsequent resurrections.

The incident unfortunately points at that we have to be more careful in our dealings with NSA. The most loving thing we can do is to prevent them from harming themselves by harming us, which we can do only by avoiding them. Jesus reminds us:

> "An ancient lesson is not overcome by the opposing of the new and old. It is not vanquished that the truth be known, nor fought against to lose to truth's appeal. There is no battle that must be prepared; no time to be expended, and no plans that need be laid for bringing in the new. There _is_ an ancient battle being waged against the truth, <u>but truth does not respond</u>. Who could be hurt in such a war, unless he hurts himself? He has no enemy in truth."
>
> (T-31.II.1)

Reading John's last blog entry made me feel envious: to have reached a point when you don't any longer have to keep watch over your ego tendencies all the time... But, reading his blog also strengthened my resolve to continue to practice. I regard John as belonging to the group ACIM calls "good teachers":

> "All good teachers realize that only fundamental change will last, but they do not begin at that level. Strengthening motivation for change is their first and foremost goal. It is also their last and final one.

> Increasing motivation for change in the learner is all that a teacher need do to guarantee change. Change in motivation is a change of mind, and this will inevitably produce fundamental change because the mind _is_ fundamental."
> (T-6.V.B.2)

And speaking of resolve, our common resolve here at the Center to continue practicing space-time-jump visualization really got boosted after having read John's account of how he discovered it himself in 2040. Having access to his and others' expertise will hopefully "get us there" faster than the more than a hundred years it took for the people at the Reykjavik Center to make their first space-time jumps.

Still, I feel humble – I haven't even come near the point which in the Bull poem in John's blog is called "The Entrance of the Deep Secret".
But, do not interpret my humbleness as resignation, only as being realistic in knowing that striving towards a goal like ours requires receptiveness, openness, persistent discipline and patience.

I pray for myself, and therefore for you all:

Stairway   Lars Gimstedt

"Our Father, let us see the face of Christ instead of our mistakes. For we who are Your holy Son are sinless.

We would look upon our sinlessness, for guilt proclaims that we are not Your Son.

And we would not forget You longer. We are lonely here, and long for Heaven, where we are at home."
(From Lesson 223)

Until next time, with love

Lena Adamson

~.~.~.~. * .~.~.~.~

January 18, 2348.
BLOG ENTRY:
Man Forgotten – The Mission.

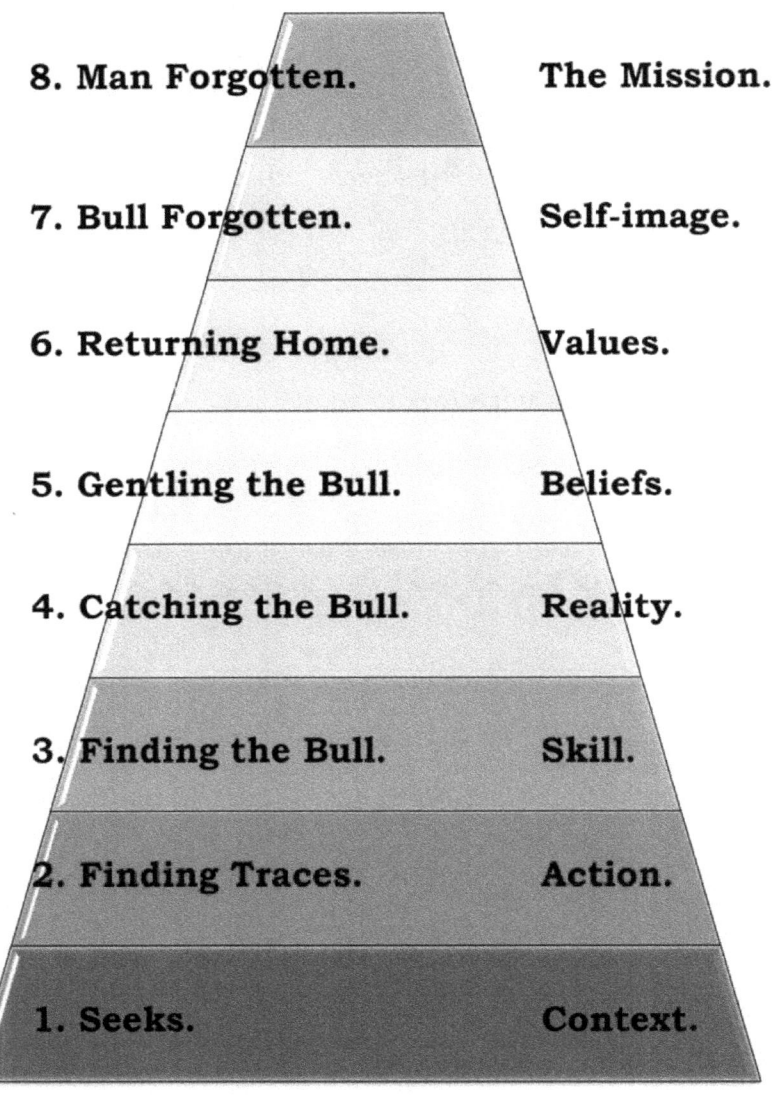

Stairway   Lars Gimstedt

Hello everyone, my Brothers and Sisters!

Since my last blog entry, the Moon Imagine Peace Tower has been installed, and it started November 25. Many of you have asked: yes it was my idea, and I am happy to report that the programming of the beam works beautifully, which all of you residing at the centers have reported.

Many have also asked how I could visualize the Moon Base sufficiently to relocate there, as I had never been there before. The answer is that I used the VR studio at our Center, and VR cameras set up by the Moon Base people at the indoors location just below the Tower installation. I used this equipment for all preparation meetings we had regarding the inauguration and start-up, so I became very familiar with the premises as well as with the people there. This is the same technique I have used with most of the other Stairway centers I have visited.

We managed to disturb NSA so much with this "trip", that a number of their scientists have now become members, and they are now deeply involved in discussions around ACIMs description of what is real and what is mental projection.

We have had a massive media coverage, where many call the latest Imagine Peace Tower "Stairway's celestial light mass", which really is an apt description – I think many use the ten minutes' of rainbow light for a moment of contemplation.

The Christmas message that we spread in all world media on Christmas Day, was well received and has rendered millions of new members, just in the last week of last year, and new seekers are continuing to sign up in large numbers.

The message was Lesson 360:

> *Peace be to me, the holy Son of God.*
>
> *Peace to my brother, who is one with me.*
>
> *Let all the world be blessed with peace through us.*

Centering oneself

But, to now continue with the story of how I found *my* Inner Peace:

During the years from 2040 to 2043 I continued to teach, hold seminars and meet with the leaders of the world.

My daily morning meditations almost always included

> *Lesson 271. Christ's is the vision I will use today.*
>
> *Lesson 276. The Word of God is given me to speak.*

These lessons helped me to focus on what my Mission was, here on Earth.

I did not travel much, despite my new-found ability to do so through space-time jumps, as it felt more and more like my mission was starting to be fulfilled.

Stairway   Lars Gimstedt

I really enjoyed just being at and around the Center on Videy, being with my friends there, and being outdoors when the weather was warm. Even if my health was good, I was in my high 90's, and could allow myself just to be, to give myself ample leisure time.

I meditated a lot on what ACIM calls the last step. How when I come to the point where I can totally let go of my identification with being a separate consciousness dwelling in a body, I will be able to let God lead me to experience Truth.

I meditated on the eighth image of The Bull and His Herdsman:

It seemed to me that this image tried to depict what is beyond all images, beyond all thoughts. I longed being in an inner state described by one of the poems under the image:

> *Space shattered at one blow*
> *and holy and worldly both vanished.*

Stairway

Lars Gimstedt

In the Untreadable the path has come to an end.

The bright moon over the temple and the sound of the wind in the tree.

*All rivers, returning their waters,
flow back again to the sea.*

The Fisherman

One night late in the year of 2043 I had a very vivid dream, which was so lucid that I could remember it as if it had happened in real life. Normally, my memories of my dreams were fuzzy, and what I remembered from them soon disappeared. But this dream I can recall in its smallest details, even today:

> *I am walking along the ocean, on a beach stretching forwards as long as I can see. Far away, I can see a person, standing alone, looking out at the sea. Coming nearer, I see that it is a man, clad in a white tunic and trousers, simple sandals on his feet. He has a belt made of a thin rope. It seems to me that the rope can mean that he is a fisherman.*
>
> *"You have made a long walk" he says, turning towards me. I immediately feel complete trust in him, meeting his calm eyes and gentle smile. "Let us sit down, and talk."*
>
> *And we walk up to a white-washed log, washed ashore by the sea, and we sit down on it, facing the ocean, and we talk.*

Stairway
Lars Gimstedt

> *He tells me that I will return home in the near future, but that my journey is not finished. He says that he wants me to go back, at a later time, to complete the task that has been planned for me. He says "I have told others before you, and I now tell you: you have an important role in the celestial speed-up of the Atonement. When you have fulfilled your part, we will meet again."*
>
> *And he gently touched my arm, and I could feel his strong hand hold my arm in what felt like a reassurance, and suddenly I was alone again, with the sound of the surf.*

And when I awoke in the morning, recalling the dream so clearly as if I really had travelled away during the night to that beach, I also remembered that I had seen the words "celestial speed-up" somewhere. I searched my e-book library, and found the words in a book describing Helen Schucman, the scribe of ACIM, and her personal journey. How she at a point in the "meetings" she had with Jesus asked why ACIM was channeled to her at that very time, to which he had answered:

> *The world situation is worsening to an alarming degree. People all over the world are being called on to help, and are making their individual contributions as part of an overall prearranged plan. (...)*
> *Because of the acute emergency however, the usual slow, evolutionary process is being bypassed in what might best be described as a 'celestial speed-up.'*

Emptying the mind

In my morning meditation that day, I returned to The Bull, to the image "Both Bull and Man Forgotten", trying to really empty my mind with the help of the image, and with the "instruction" underneath:

When all worldly desires have dropped away, holiness, too, has lost its meaning.

Do not stay at a place where Buddha is, and quickly pass by where he is not.

Not even a thousand eyes can see into the heart of one who clings to neither.

Holiness to which birds consecrate flowers is shameful.

The dream, and meditating on what the Fisherman said, and meditating on the empty circle, made me understand that my continued mission depended on my forgetting not only my thoughts but also "forgetting", letting go of, all my concepts of who I had thought I was. To really let The Holy Spirit define not only what to do, but also define who I am: A Son of God and a Messenger for His Words.

Or more correctly, let The Holy Spirit *remind* me who I always have been, and what I deepest down in my mind really want to do, being that.

Opening the mind

Looking back on the period that followed this dream, I now realize what I do not think I was aware of at the time: even if I remained present in person at the Center on Iceland, I was probably seen as very absent-minded. I preferred to be by myself, and I participated in fewer and fewer official gatherings at the Center, even if I still met personally with many of the guests, many of them world leaders in high positions.

When the weather was warm I took long, albeit slow, walks around Videy. But instead of climbing up to the top of the island, I now preferred to walk along the shore, now and then sitting down on a stone or a log, and just meditate on the vast ocean: always the same and always changing. How the water could change appearance from very still to breaking surf, how it's color changed with the color of the sky, with the position of the sun, with the weather.

A perfect image of the mind. Including the fact that deeper down there are invisible but strong under-currents. And at the bottom, the ocean is perfectly still all the time and has the same temperature, all around the year.

Stairway — Lars Gimstedt

My meditation object during that time was always the empty circle. I felt that I was "releasing my grip of the earthly reality", but I did not ever have a sense of loss. I was not confused in any way, and I could always "return" when needed, to be with my wife, and with my children and grandchildren when they visited us, or to participate in meetings, and so on. But, mostly I was absent from "this world", on my way home, even if I also knew that I was asked to return here again, sometimes in the future.

> *Whip and rein, bull and man, are all gone and vanished.*
>
> *No words can encompass the blue vault of the sky.*
>
> *How could snow pile up on a red-hot hearth?*
>
> *Only when arrived at this place*
> *can a man match the old masters.*

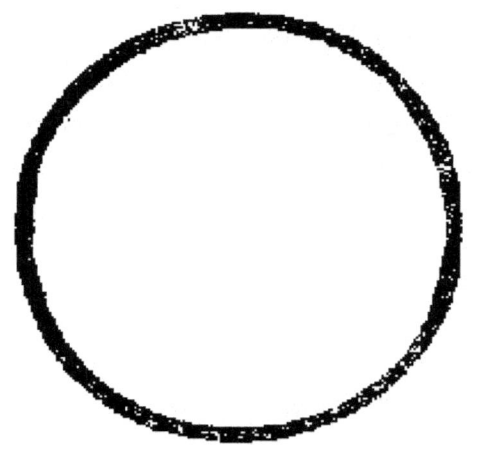

I interpreted "the old masters", as those Teachers of God before me that had attained what ACIM in Manual for Teachers describes as "open-mindedness":

> *The centrality of open-mindedness, perhaps the last of the attributes the teacher of God acquires, is easily understood when its relation to forgiveness is recognized. (...)*
>
> *How do the open-minded forgive? They have let go all things that would prevent forgiveness. <u>They have in truth abandoned the world</u>, and let it be restored to them in newness and in joy so glorious they could never have conceived of such a change. Nothing is now as it was formerly. Nothing but sparkles now which seemed so dull and lifeless before. And above all are all things welcoming, for threat is gone. No clouds remain to hide the face of Christ.*
>
> *Now is the goal achieved. Forgiveness is the final goal of the curriculum. It paves the way for what goes far beyond all learning. The curriculum makes no effort to exceed its legitimate goal. Forgiveness is its single aim, at which all learning ultimately converges.*
>
> *It is indeed enough.*
>
> *(M-4.X.1.)*

I really felt that I had reached the inner state described in Lesson 273:

Stairway

The stillness of the peace of God is mine.

Perhaps we are now ready for a day of undisturbed tranquility. If this is not yet feasible, we are content and even more than satisfied to learn how such a day can be achieved. If we give way to a disturbance, let us learn how to dismiss it and return to peace. We need but tell our minds, with certainty, "The stillness of the peace of God is mine," and nothing can intrude upon the peace that God Himself has given to His Son.

Father, Your peace is mine. What need have I to fear that anything can rob me of what You would have me keep?
I cannot lose Your gifts to me. And so the peace You gave Your Son is with me still, in quietness and in my own eternal love for You.

January 22, 2348. NSA Report.

```
*************************
```
NSA Report 2346-1001-4545
TOP SECRET. CLF code 0.
<u>REQUEST FOR ACTION</u>.
Department for The Transhuman Threat.
January 30 2348.
Unmonitored disappearances.
Case study TTT-JZ-1.
```
*************************
```

JZ's last blog entry revealed that he had actually planned his return in September 19 2346 before he disappeared 2046, although he did not reveal the time to his staff.

His account of "getting instructions" via a dream cannot be interpreted in any other way as an attempt to make the followers of his sect believe in divine intervention, thereby masking his real intentions: acquiring power over people's minds.

His talk about "old masters", insinuating that he is one himself, can only be seen as the typical megalomania of a sect leader.

The number of TSS disconnects have been rapidly increasing after Jan 1 from a couple per month worldwide to hundreds per day. Approximately 25% of these have not reappeared, or have not triggered reconnect on the TSS. Major revisions of the TSS system has been rendered necessary, to keep up the records of the increasing numbers of un-tracked individuals, something the system had not originally been prepared to do. Similar revisions have been implemented in other data base systems as well, as banking, finance, insurance, etc.

In order to protect the integrity of NSA-TTT, we have arrested and isolated a number of defected NSA people, both agents, scientific experts and former managers. A few of these have been able to utilize neuroportation to free themselves, but the majority have not done this.

We have forced the remaining ones into an intense program for mental re-programming. These programs have been used for almost 350 years, and have been refined to a 97% positive yield. Strangely enough, there have been no effects whatsoever on our new subjects, not even the usual initial rages and hysterical fits. On the contrary, these subjects have managed to maintain their odd equanimity. This new type of brainwash does not seem to correspond to any known psychological theory.

In addition, they have exerted some kind of influence, probably by BQRF, on our interrogators and psychologists, which have resulted in the defection of three psychologists to Stairway.

To prevent this "infiltration by proxy", we have now terminated the program for arrests of former NSA employees, and we have limited the contacts with the confined subjects to communication via hubots.

To summarize the issue of NSA-TTT integrity, we are forced to report that it is in severe danger. We lack sufficient number of agents, and have to compensate with automated surveillance, which gives many erroneous feed-backs due to the irregularities of the surveilled Stairway subjects. We also lack a sufficient number of experts, and in some fields of investigation we have had to put a number of programs in hold.

Together with the fact that a large number of nations have stopped all co-operation with NSA-TTT and confiscated our equipment, we have to issue a severe warning: if new resources are not added, WE RISK LOSING CONTROL ALTOGETHER, something that has not even been a thinkable risk the last 300 years.

<u>We demand immediate action from top level NSA!</u>

****
End of NSA Report 2346-1001-4545
TOP SECRET. CLF code 0. <u>REQUEST FOR ACTION</u>.
January 30 2348.
****

Stairway   Lars Gimstedt

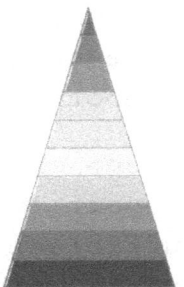

January 30, 2348.
Stairway New Zealand News.

Dear Sisters and Brothers

First a reminder: Next Moon Tower meditation will be now on Tuesday February 3 at 8:30 PM, <u>this time in Auckland Sports Stadium</u>. The ones that we have had, the first December 3 and the second on January 3, were wonderful experiences, with clear weather and no wind. So beautiful, seeing the sequence of Stairway colors. We were lucky to have such fine weather, as we were many more people attending than had been possible to get into our auditorium.

For the coming one, the city of Auckland will sponsor the meditation, which as I said above will be at the Sports Stadium.

Stairway

Lars Gimstedt

The two former NSA agents that joined us last summer were arrested by NSA December 27, despite our efforts to protect them. But I am happy to report that they were released again, after only a couple of days' interrogation and attempts to get them to change their minds about Stairway, which NSA calls "a brainwashing sect". Our friends were surprised though — they knew NSA as always having had a professional and tough atmosphere, but they now experienced their former colleagues as nervous, describing them as "fidgety", and they had most of the time been physically separated from NSA personnel, communicating only by VR com. They have no idea about what is going on at the local NSA base, but they experienced it as if there is some kind of internal crisis.

~.~. * .~.~

To John's last blog entry, this time about the period when he was 94 to 97, a period when most people look back on their lives, usually with both regret and gratefulness.

John on the other hand still looked forward, still wanting his life's mission to unfold. But he had come to the point in his spiritual journey where his "inner work" was finalized. Instead, he stopped himself, centered himself in the Eternal Now, and waited.

And "The Fisherman" came to him and told him to prepare to "go home", but not as the final step of his journey but as the last giant step to his final task here on Earth. And John, having truly learned that we are to be intermediaries for the Power of God, prepared himself by emptying his mind completely. He had, as he used an ACIM quote to describe, "in truth abandoned the world, and let it be restored in newness and in joy".

It is with fascination and in awe I read the description of what I understand must be John's last steps towards complete enlightenment. It feels both so simple and so impossible for "me as an ordinary human being" to attain. But, luckily both my meetings with John and reading his "travel log" have convinced me that he is (or at least once was) an ordinary human being, and what he has accomplished, all of us can.

With the maybe little depressing addition: after a lot of disciplined work...

But about the feeling of awe, even Jesus reminds us:

Stairway — Lars Gimstedt

"Equals should not be in awe of one another because awe implies inequality. It is therefore an inappropriate reaction to me. An elder brother is entitled to respect for his greater experience, and obedience for his greater wisdom. He is also entitled to love because he is a brother, and to devotion if he is devoted. It is only my devotion that entitles me to yours.

There is nothing about me that you cannot attain. I have nothing that does not come from God. The difference between us now is that I have nothing else. This leaves me in a state which is only potential in you."

(T-1.II.3)

Until next time, with love

Lena Adamson

~.~.~.~. * .~.~.~.~

March 21, 2348.
BLOG ENTRY: The Origin – The Vision.

Step	Aspect
9. The Origin.	The Vision.
8. Man Forgotten.	The Mission.
7. Bull Forgotten.	Self-image.
6. Returning Home.	Values.
5. Gentling the Bull.	Beliefs.
4. Catching the Bull.	Reality.
3. Finding the Bull.	Skill.
2. Finding Traces.	Action.
1. Seeks.	Context.

Stairway Lars Gimstedt

Lesson 291. This is a day of stillness and of peace.

Lesson 300. Only an instant does this world endure.

With these lessons from ACIM, I welcome you, dear Brothers and Sisters, to the blog of your humble servant Senior Adviser John Zacharias.

Even if NSA-TTT are not promoting neither stillness nor peace, with their massive arrests all over the world, it is my sincere hope and my request that you remember to forgive them, and to see their actions as subconscious calls for help.

Because, as soon as you counter-attack in any way, even if only in your private thoughts, you will be attacking yourself and you will lose contact with your Inner Peace.

<u>If</u> you truly want to help them – they are also Brothers and Sisters, although this thought is still alien to them – <u>the only way</u> you can ever help them is by remaining in your Inner Peace and in a firm belief that no one of us in Stairway has really been harmed in any way.

More and more people outside of the Stairway Movement are coming to our help. Much of this help is unfortunately counter-productive (forgive them for this!), but much is good, and contributes to World Peace, which is a notion more and more people, more and more of the media, are talking about as an actual possibility.

We welcome the fact that Tibet has been granted autonomy from China. They were the first to close

Stairway Lars Gimstedt

down NSA activities within their borders, something that has been repeated by many other nations.
I have had discussions with a number of world leaders that seem to contemplate doing the same, saying that they realize that the former NSA-enforced policies for security may have produced in_security, both for their inhabitants and for the political system.

An increasing number of these leaders have expressed that they have changed their vision on how to achieve World Peace. The Vision which is starting to evolve essentially says: *"When Inner Peace is a natural state of all, World Peace will follow."* Many of them even use concepts from ACIM, maybe without even being aware of this, when they say *"As long as people perceive the world as a place of lack and danger, there can be no lasting peace."*

More about The Vision, in the part below where I will continue with the story of my personal journey, now the last period before I went Home for a while, the years 2043 to 2046.

But first, some advice around the issue of going Home. Many of you have had friends and relatives that have disappeared, and that have not returned. I know you grieve them, and that the loss hurts. But I also hope that you know where they have gone, and that you are open to the thought that you will, when the pain has subsided, feel happy for them.

Many of you may be on your way towards a transition yourself. And here comes my advice: The authorities have implemented a number of new regulations and laws leading to the confiscation of material and financial belongings of disappeared people, which has affected spouses, children and relatives in negative ways. If you know that transition is a possibility for you, ask The Holy Spirit for guidance on what to do with what you own. Even if material goods may feel meaningless to you, they might be helpful on the continued journey of your loved ones. It may be a good idea to prepare gift certificates as required, and ask your loved ones to safe-keep them until needed.

Holding on to the Vision

Back to the story of my journey: The years 2043 to 2046.

Mankind was struggling more and more with the still increasing average temperature of the world due to the green-house effect that also was further increased by the bitter wars that broke out between many nations over scarce resources. Despite all this, I could maintain my constant sense of Inner Peace.

More and more climate refugees that had started to flee from nations inside the +-45 degree latitude band caused worldwide civil unrest. To all countries in northern Europe, Asia and North America, as well as Siberia, Greenland and Inuit, millions immigrants came each year.

But, my sense of peace was not a way of closing myself off from all this, or a way of rationalizing it away as being illusory. On the contrary, I was convinced that the environmental and social problems of the world *had* to be solved, in order to make it altogether possible for people to even contemplate developing spiritually. Health, peace and ecological balance were crucial, lest mankind would revert back into ego-dominated barbarism.

I knew that *"we go to Heaven all together, or not at all"*.

One of the books from the early phases of my own spiritual journey came to my mind, "Being Peace" by Thich Nhat Hanh, in which he describes the "Three Gems" of Buddhism:

1. Buddha, the awakened One.
2. Dharma, the way of understanding and loving.
3. Sangha, the community that lives in harmony and awareness.

Sangha sounded very much like ACIM's "The Happy Dream", the state of mankind just before all awake to the Knowledge of who they really are, God's Children, One with Him.

In talking about the first two, he furthermore writes:

> *I like to use the example of a small boat crossing the Gulf of Siam. In Vietnam, there are many people, called boat people, who leave the country in small boats. Often the boats are caught in*

Stairway

Lars Gimstedt

rough seas or storms, the people may panic, and boats can sink.

But if even one person aboard can remain calm, lucid, knowing what to do and what not to do, he or she can help the boat survive. His or her expression - face, voice - communicates clarity and calmness, and people have trust in that person. They will listen to what he or she says. One such person can save the lives of many.

Our world is something like a small boat. Compared with the cosmos, our planet is a very small boat. We are about to panic because our situation is no better than the situation of the small boat in the sea. You know that we have more than 50,000 nuclear weapons. Humankind has become a very dangerous species.

We need people who can sit still and be able to smile, who can walk peacefully. We need people like that in order to save us. Mahayana Buddhism says that you are that person, that each of you is that person.

So, I was convinced that I could help by maintaining my Inner Peace, and help better than if I had felt frustration, anger, or felt critical, even if these emotions were "natural" and "justified" in the situation the world had created for itself.

I met with many world leaders in this period, in long private discussions. I found that everyone I met was striving to find solutions - technical, organizational, financial, juridical and social. I found this attitude both in the pragmatic ones, with no conscious spiritual interests, as in those that were very spiritually advanced.

I felt we all shared the same Vision: despite all negative appearances, it is possible to create a better world.

And I knew that my contribution, even if it was not much on a practical or concrete level, was important: to maintain and to communicate this Vision, and to communicate my trust in that by just a little willingness, The Holy Spirit in everyone will ultimately come through and be heard.

I knew that *"people who can sit still and be able to smile, who can walk peacefully"* are needed, even when they do "nothing more".

Returning to the Origin

In my daily meditations, I had now switched to the ninth image in The Bull and His Herdsman – "Return to the Origin, Back to the Source" :

Stairway Lars Gimstedt

In the origin all is pure and there is no dust.

Collected in the peace of 'wu-wei', the wonderful action of non-action where all wilful doing has ceased, he beholds the coming and going of all things.

No longer deluded by shifting phantom pictures, he has nothing further to learn.

Blue runs the river, green range the mountains; he sits by himself and beholds the change of all things.

And I somehow knew, that I longer needed to "be vigilant for His Kingdom", as my ego had receded completely. I no longer needed to remind myself of who I was – not only acting as a messenger but embodying, *being*, the Message. I could just let my Inner Light shine outwards, dispelling shadows, enabling others to see more clearly.

And because of this, even whilst listening to all the problems, seeing disasters on TV, I could breathe calmly, when others felt choked. I could smile gently, when others felt despair and hopelessness. I could walk peacefully, when other ran frantically around. And by doing this, making miracles possible.

> *The great activity does not pander to*
> *being or not being.*
>
> *And so, to see and to hear he need not be*
> *as one deaf and blind.*
>
> *Last night the golden bird flew down into the sea,*
>
> *Yet today as of old,*
> *the red ring of dawn flares up in the sky.*

***

Saying good-bye

I had another lucid dream, just after the summer of 2046.

In the dream I again met the Fisherman, and as in the previous dream we sat down on the sea-washed log. The ocean was almost completely calm, only small waves licked our bare feet that we had put into the water, which felt warm and soft. He said: *"This time, you have remained still, in the same place, but you have advanced further than you ever have done before."*

And we talked for a long period of time. About my journey that had started sixty years earlier, about each important step I had taken on my journey. About how this journey had been a gradual discovery

Stairway

of my true identity, a journey of Self-realization. And how I had let the Voice of the Self, The Holy Spirit, come through more and more.

And how all this had affected my self-image as well as how I regarded God. From total repression, through fear, and finally to complete Trust and Love.

Finally, he asked me to prepare for jumping in time. He told me that I would have to leave everybody I knew and loved, and that I would come back the same place and the very same day three hundred years into the future. He wanted me to let this happen on my coming birthday, my 100:th.

He explained to me that I should tell everyone dependent on me in any way about my departure, but he said that I should not reveal anything about when I was going to return, only that I would return after more than an average human lifespan.

As in our previous encounter, he took hold of my arm reassuringly, and disappeared.

I awoke, and it was in the middle of the night. I could hear my wife Hi'ilani breathing quietly besides me in our bed. I first felt shocked, even terrified, my heart beat as rapid as if I had been running at top speed. But thanks to my long training I just let the emotions be, without trying to change them. I recognized them as my natural, automatic reaction to meeting sudden change unprepared, the old engineer in me craving previous notice and concrete action plans.

Stairway — Lars Gimstedt

Through just observing my emotions and thoughts, without judging them or trying to control them, they finally abated, and I could start to think clearly again.

I understood that many would interpret my upcoming "permanent" disappearance as death. Not Hi'ilani, as she had come very far in her own spiritual development, and not most of my friends at the Centers. But nevertheless, they would certainly be shocked, they would become frightened and they would grieve.

And at this thought, grief came to me. For a long while, maybe several hours, I silently cried at the realization of that I would never again see my loved ones – Hi'ilani, our children, our nine grandchildren, my close friends all over the world.

At dawn I had calmed myself some. I still felt an intense sorrow, but at the same time I knew deep inside that beyond time and space we would all meet again. This did not make me feel less sorry, but it gave me energy to act.

I knew that my departure had to be prepared, and that there now were a lot of things I would need to do. In the days that followed, after having told Hi'ilani and my family of my coming departure, I worked on a very practical and concrete level together with my staff at the Center. We secured the financial security of my family, and we prepared all the paperwork to the authorities and to the NSA, in order to minimize disturbances to the Stairway Movement.

Stairway Lars Gimstedt

As I had foreseen, Hi'ilani first became very upset, and we had many long talks together. She tried first to press me about when I was going to return, but she understood after a while that this information could be misused by others, and she accepted that it would be a long period, and that she would not see me again, at least not on Earth. As we had a little more than a month to use, we could plan in good ways for our children and their families to come to Iceland, and they arrived in the course of the next couple of weeks. Together, we wrote my "testament", which summarized which authority paperwork that we had to prepare, and which described our plans for the coming month, and when and how my departure would be.

After things had calmed down a bit, I even had time to return to just being with myself, taking long walks, meditating.

I took the time to review my second lucid dream about my encounter with the Fisherman, and I summarized what we had talked about regarding my inner journey during sixty years, and I put together the following table:

Stairway Lars Gimstedt

Step	Context	Developed	Self-image	God
1 Seeks	Conflict	Discipline	Engineer...	Invisible
2 Traces	Action	Patience	I can grow.	Allowing
3 Finds	Skills	Awareness	I am OK.	Creative
4 Catches	Reality	Acceptance	I want.	Inspiring
5 Gentles	Beliefs	Self-worth	I am human.	Compassion
6 Returns	Values	Forgiveness	I am needed.	Wisdom
7 Forgets	Self-image	Love	I am kind.	Loving
8 Releases	The Mission	Perception	I am whole.	Embracing
9 Origin	The Vision	Peace	I am perfect.	Everywhere

I could see that the Fisherman had used the same structure I had been using all the years, the Ten Bull Images, when we had talked about the different steps I had taken.

Seeing the table was like an awakening in itself – recalling everything that had happened. Putting it into the structure of the table, it really felt like I had been guided, even if I had not been consciously aware of this in the beginning. It also felt like the guidance seemed to have had followed a plan, defined in advance.

And I realized that the next step, which would probably come after returning to Earth three hundred years from the day of my departure, could maybe be characterized by the title of the tenth and final Bull image: *"Entering the Market-place with Bliss-bestowing Hands"*.

This made me feel a bit elated and also very curious: what was I supposed to do? What would the world look like three hundred years from now? Would the Stairway Movement still exist?

Stairway — Lars Gimstedt

I had a thousand questions, and longed for having another lucid dream, in which I could ask the Fisherman all these questions, but I never had any more dream during my last time period at the Stairway Center on Videy, in the fall of 2046.

Leaving

On the day September 19 2046, the day of my birthday, everyone had prepared everything to be as normal as possible.

I woke early in the morning by my family singing outside our bedroom door, and they entered as many birthdays before with breakfast. And with one present only, as I had not planned to bring much with me to the future. Hi'ilani had bought a gemstone that originated from Mars, a geode gray and rough on the outside, beautifully glimmering on the inside. It had been sliced into two halves that could be put together, forming the original gray stone. She said it was to be a symbol of my own discovery of my Self inside, and a reminder to see it in all others I was going to meet.

Stairway
Lars Gimstedt

I was pleased to see that it also had the rainbow colors of the Stairway logo, with purple crystals symbolizing Oneness in the center.

After being together for a couple of hours in our apartment, we all went to the big auditorium of the Center, where everyone at the Center had gathered.

Here my friends had arranged a big fare-well party, with snacks and drinks, and I spent the next two hours mingling, talking with each one of them. I met with both tears and smiles, both calmness and anxiety, but the atmosphere was still dominated by anticipation and joy.

I had decided to depart at noon, and one hour before we all sat down on meditation mats, cushions or stools, and I led a group meditation on the word Peace.

When everyone was well into the final visualization, I went into my own visualization, as many times before, of a specific place on the shore on the northwest point of Videy, and I made my transit there, 300 years forward in time.

I opened my eyes, and saw to my relief that everything looked exactly as usual. The weather was warm, the ocean breeze from southwest brought with it the usual scents from the fishing harbor in Reykjavik.

I checked in my handbag that my gemstone was there. I checked my communicator, which reported that there was no contact with the net, but that the

Stairway

GPS network still worked. This felt reassuring – mankind was still there...

I rose and started to walk back to the Center, which I could see in the distance.

Stairway — Lars Gimstedt

March 25, 2348. NSA Report.

****

```
NSA Report 2346-1001-4667
TOP SECRET. CLF code 0.
Department for The Transhuman Threat.
March 25 2348.
Unmonitored disappearances.
Case study TTT-JZ-1.
```

****

JZ disappeared after his last blog entry March 21, but the structure of his blog indicates that there will be at least one more. TSS has been armed to detect his reappearance, even on the Moon Base and on the Mars bases.

The blog revealed the existence of a "testament" made by JZ 2046, and obviously it was written on paper with a fountain pen (a writing device used before the 19th century) and stored only in physical form, therefore not detected by the TSS system. It has now been retrieved by NSA agents. In the testament, JZ informed about his plan for disappearance and return, although no date for the latter was given.

To date twenty-three countries have closed down the TSS system within their borders, resulting in large global security gaps.

Stairway

Lars Gimstedt

High-level negotiations are ongoing at UN, to restore TSS.

Tibet belongs to these countries. They closed down TSS days after their autonomy from China was established. The Lhasa Stairway Center has increased its membership numbers very rapidly, and 67 % of the population of Tibet are now Stairway members.

In the absence of clear instructions from UN and NSA, and also due to conflicting instructions from different parts of NSA top management, NSA-TTT has decided to become an autonomous organization. As a result, FBI have been making arrests of our agents, forcing us to relocate to secret locations on other continents than North America.

From today, these report will be distributed internally NSA-TTT only.

The authors of this report belong to a relocated office, and we now experience improved efficiency in pursuing security measures deemed necessary. But, with less authority liaison, the security focus has been changed to the integrity of the NSA-TTT organization itself, instead of securing the security of government institutions.

****

Stairway   Lars Gimstedt

```
End of NSA Report 2346-1001-4667
TOP SECRET. CLF code 0.
March 25 2348.

*************************
```

Stairway   Lars Gimstedt

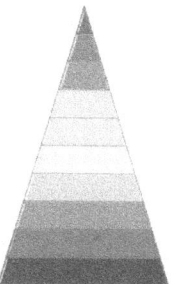

March 30, 2348.
Stairway New Zealand News.

Dear Sisters and Brothers

It is hard to believe, but John Z seems to believe it: the ancient dream about World Peace can actually become fulfilled in our time! It seems that he and the Reykjavik Center are playing an important role in this.

John's transit somewhere after his last blog entry March 21 is probably connected with these efforts. They have not informed us where to and to which point in time, but I will inform you as soon as I know anything more about this.

World Peace... My "old mind" keeps telling me "that's impossible, wake up to reality, you fool!". But my "new mind" tells me to listen to Jesus saying

Stairway Lars Gimstedt

> "Miracles are natural.
> When they do not occur
> something has gone wrong."
> (The sixth Miracle Principle, T-1.I.6)

And what has "gone wrong" *is* the old mind.

Things are happening rapidly in our "quiet corner" of the Earth as well: an increasing number of New Zealanders have learned to jump in space-time, and a few seem to have made their final transit Home.

A humbling fact is that none of us here at the Center have yet achieved the transit ability, but we are really inspired into doubling our efforts in practicing...

John's advice about preparing oneself before going Home at first felt to me like a conflict between staying in the illusion and waking up to Reality, but after a while I realized that this preparation in itself is a part of the Awakening. Arranging economy and possessions for one's loved ones is an act of Love towards Brothers and Sisters not yet fully awakened. To make their lives as secure as possible will help them focus on the important task they have in front of them: first to change their old dream to The Happy Dream, then ultimately to wake up from the dream all together.

To want to help your loved ones is of course still a part of "special relationships", which ACIM says belong to "the old mind", but here you can let The Holy Spirit <u>use</u> your special relationships as a tool for the Atonement:

> "It is no dream to love your brother as yourself. Nor is your holy relationship a dream. All that remains of dreams within it is that it is still a special relationship. Yet it is very useful to the Holy Spirit, Who has a special function here. It will become the happy dream through which He can spread joy to thousands on thousands who believe that love is fear, not happiness. Let Him fulfill the function that He gave to your relationship by accepting it for you, and nothing will be wanting that would make of it what He would have it be." (T-18.V.5)

Stairway Lars Gimstedt

But now, let us go back to John's story. In his last blog entry he describes his last period on Earth 300 years ago, the three last years before his jump to our time.

John's quote from the Buddhist monk Thich Nhat Hahn, the parable about the boat in a storm, is a vivid reminder of the acute crisis the world faced at that time. We tend to forget this, in our present time of force field weather control from the Equatorial Satellite Ring and unlimited clean energy from our fusion reactors. And the crisis probably contributed as an important part of John's spiritual training, to manage in keeping his state of Inner Peace in the extreme turmoil around him...

One of the poems from the ninth Bull picture, one that John did not include in his blog, I think describes John's ability to be "blind and deaf" to the unreal rather well:

> "Done is what has to be done,
> and all ways are completed.
>
> Clearest awakening does not differ
> from being blind and deaf.
>
> The way he once came has ended
> under his straw sandals.

Stairway
Lars Gimstedt

> *No bird sings.*
> *Red flowers glow in crimson splendor."*

He describes how he manages to maintain his Inner Peace by holding on to his Vision, and in doing this he had returned to "The Origin", using the symbol in the book about "The Bull" — "In the origin all is pure and there is no dust."

His vision was "Despite all appearances of the opposite, it is possible to create a better world". He says he shared this vision with many of the world leaders at the time, although I don't think their vision included one important part of John's vision, the attainment of "The Happy Dream" – World Peace.

It was fascinating to read about John's second encounter with the Fisherman. The description of what happened resembles more the many stories in the Bible of visions prophets and others received in dreams, than the experience Helen Schucman had when receiving the text of ACIM. But, disregarding how these divine interventions happen or are experienced, or are made

Stairway Lars Gimstedt

into form by the receiving mind, the very notion of divine intervention makes me feel awe and gratefulness.

John's sharing of his sorrow in knowing that he would never see his loved ones again after his coming time-jump moved me deeply, especially now when I know many of you have had the same experience that John's wife Hi'ilani and his children had, three hundred years ago.

It felt good reading how he prepared his transit, and how talking with everyone involved, his family and people at the Center, led to a gathering that sounded more like a celebration than a funeral.
Of course, all there knew that it was not death, but still, it was losing him forever.

For us now, in this time, it is <u>only</u> celebration - thanks to Jesus' work from year 35 or so, through recurring interventions during more than two thousand three hundred years (which although is less than 1% of the age of our race, Homo Sapiens), we are now nearer World Peace than ever before! And in addition to Jesus, we should also be grateful to all the Miracle Worker and God's Teachers that have taken on these roles thanks to ACIM and other divine messages. Specifically, I feel

Stairway   Lars Gimstedt

grateful for John's dedication and persistence in following _his_ calling, that came unexpectedly to him in the middle of his life, and that made him to become one of the most prominent Teachers.

A celebration although shadowed by "counterattacks" from ego-mindedness in the world, so I want to remind you again: try to see disruptive or destructive actions from authorities, from certain conservative or fundamentalist groups, from other individuals, as subconscious calls for love, and answer with love and forgiveness only. But love can also be to stop others from harming themselves by attacking others, so as far as you can, protect yourselves by keeping away from exposed locations, by keeping information in safe places, and so on.

Jesus reminds us:

> "But forget not this: When you become disturbed and lose your peace of mind because another is attempting to solve his problems through fantasy, you are refusing to forgive yourself for just this same attempt. And you are holding both of you away from truth and from salvation. As you forgive him, you restore to truth what was denied

by both of you. And you will see forgiveness where you have given it."

(T-17.I.6)

I am really looking forward to John's return and to his next blog entry, in which I hope he will tell us about what has happened since he came here one and a half year ago. I don't know when he has planned next entry to come, but as soon as it has come, I will write to you again.

Until next time, with love

Lena Adamson

Stairway Lars Gimstedt

June 11, 2348. NSA Report.

****

NSA Report 2346-1001-4717
TOP SECRET. CLF code 0.
Department for The Transhuman Threat.
June 11 2348.
Unmonitored disappearances.
Case study TTT-JZ-1.

****

There is still no TSS re-connect to JZ, almost three months after his last disappearance.

The Lhasa Stairway Center triggered a massive TSS disconnect June 1, and we investigated on site the same day, with ten search experts. They found the Center completely abandoned, even by the Dalai Lhama, and we could later confirm that the whole center staff have become disconnected from TSS.

All probes have been checked and we have found no signs of tampering or sabotage. A complete list of all disappeared persons has been compiled, and TSS has been armed for rapid reconnect with coverage both globally and in space habitats, with special focus on all NSA facilities.

Stairway — Lars Gimstedt

This first mass disappearance has led to the present unrest / political crisis, which dominates media and also authority activities. There is a lot of speculations about JZ's role, but as yet no conclusions about this can be made.

We have interrogated all Tibetans deemed to have had connections with the Lhasa Center, and we get conflicting information. On one hand, they claim to know nothing about it, on the other hand they do not seem to be alarmed, shocked, grieving, or the like. Our present assumption is that the disappearance was planned in advance and that the population of Tibet, or at least large parts of it, had been informed.

We have put more resources to signal surveillance on net and com traffic, in order to catch information about more mass disappearances.

We have no contingency plan for anything like this. As the only logical and realistic plan deemed workable, NSA-TTT has decided to isolate itself completely from all liaison with national organizations, and to henceforth follow internal NSA-TTT plans only.

We have found technical solutions for immediate disabling of all communication devices carried by defected agents, experts and NSA-TTT managers, minimizing the risk for infiltration.

****

End of NSA Report 2346-1001-4717
TOP SECRET. CLF code 0.
June 11 2348.

****

Stairway   Lars Gimstedt

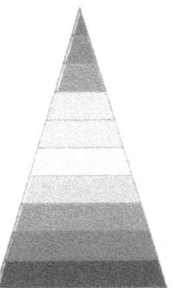

June 30, 2348.
Stairway New Zealand News.

Dear Sisters and Brothers

John Z has not returned yet, and in order to help you to assess the numerous rumors going around, we will immediately announce <u>any</u> information we get from the Main Center. As for today, there is no more information about John.

As you surely all know, the entire staff at the Lhasa Center has made their final transit Home, which has been confirmed from Main Center. We have had many informal gatherings here at the Center, where many of you have participated. We have talked about and meditated on this first collective return Home.

Understandably, it engenders mixed feelings – anxiety, insecurity, grief, but also anticipation, awe and curiosity.

Many have brought up whether this can be connected to any of the old myths about collective disappearances that have existed in many religions. For example the Christian myth about the Rapture, where God takes parts of mankind home, leaving the rest to "the Tribulation", a period for the Final Judgment of the non-believers, that if they do not convert, will be punished at the Second Coming of Christ.

Our firm belief here at our Center is that these myths belong to the thought models that perceived God as demanding and punishing, whereas ACIM claims that He cannot be, it would be a contradiction to His inherent nature.

We believe that this collective transit Home is the result of enlightenment in each person individually. When they all had reached this point in their spiritual path, there was a communion in this enlightenment, by which they reached a collective decision.

The fact that they informed the Main Center about this, before they made their Transit, also supports our belief.

Jesus says in ACIM about the Tribulation:

> "In this world you need not have tribulation because I have overcome the world. That is why you should be of good cheer."
> (T-4.I.13)

He also explains what <u>He</u> means with the Biblical terms the First and the Second Coming:

> "The First Coming of Christ is merely another name for the creation, for Christ is the Son of God.
>
> The Second Coming of Christ means nothing more than the end of the ego's rule and the healing of the mind. I was created like you in the First, and I have called you to join with me in the Second.
>
> I am in charge of the Second Coming, and my judgment, which is used only for protection, cannot be wrong because it never attacks. Yours may be so distorted that you believe I was mistaken in choosing you. I assure you this is a mistake of your ego. Do not mistake it for humility. Your ego is trying to convince you that it is real and I am not, because if I am real, I am no more real than you are. That knowledge, and I assure you that it is knowledge, means that Christ has

come into your mind and healed it."
(T-4.IV.10)

And just before Lesson 301, He explains specifically in the section "What is the Second Coming?" :

> "Christ's Second Coming, which is sure as God, is merely the correction of mistakes, and the return of sanity.
> It is a part of the condition that restores the never lost, and re-establishes what is forever and forever true.
> It is the invitation to God's Word to take illusion's place; the willingness to let forgiveness rest upon all things without exception and without reserve."

So, we who live here on Earth, are still "insane".

The good news is though than more and more of us are awakening, opening up more and more to Truth, more and more "returning to sanity".

Until next time, with love

Lena Adamson

~.~.~.~. * .~.~.~.~

Stairway   Lars Gimstedt

July 2, 2348. NSA Report.

****

NSA Report 2346-1001-4833
TOP SECRET. CLF code 0.
Department for The Transhuman Threat.
July 2 2348.
Unmonitored disappearances.
Case study TTT-JZ-1.

****

Still no re-connect to JZ. The main Stairway Center is of course involved, but other Stairway Centers also remain passive with respect to JZ's absence, which can be a sign of them having been informed in forehand. We are trying to trace any information on their internal net about his return, but to date none has been found, not even internal speculations, pointing at the fact that every center has been informed verbally or by coded messages (we have intercepted messages that self-destruct, a sign of encryption, although with a method unknown to us).

The world leader meeting at the UN, and the resolution published, stating that security forces shall be stationed at all finance and government buildings worldwide, has had a large impact on NSA activities. It has also restored the position of NSA-TTT somewhat, and we have been able to re-allocate many of our activities to our old headquarters.

But, despite the welcome addition from these security measures, new security risks have to be assessed due to the new co-operation treaty between the Asian Union, the European Union, the African Union and the Pan American Union.

TSS has been heavily upgraded with respect to data integrity, in order to be able to handle the increasing number of disconnects from disappearances, now up to thousands per day.

****

End of NSA Report 2346-1001-4833
TOP SECRET. CLF code 0.
July 2 2348.

****

Stairway   Lars Gimstedt

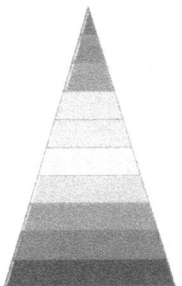

July 30, 2348.
Stairway New Zealand News.

Dear Sisters and Brothers

The fact that no extra newsletters have been published means that there is no information about John's return, except that he will return.

The increasing number of Transits has made the authorities nervous, up to the highest level, and the UN decision to increase security around all government offices has been noticeable here on New Zealand as well.

Probably coupled to this, NSA activities and interrogations of members and of us at the Center have also increased, although they have let our members that have left their NSA employment be – they even seem to avoid them.

Stairway   Lars Gimstedt

Good world news is the agreement between the unions of Asia, Europe, Africa and America.

The ego reacts with suspicion and fear when it is subjected to the True Mind. The increased surveillance and control is a sign of ego-mindedness reacting to increased "Right-mindedness", especially when it becomes evident strongly as space-time jumps, but also when it comes out in weaker forms as increased trust between nations.

But, it is important also to realize that the only thing that makes it possible for going Home is Knowledge, which we cannot attain without God's help. Right-mindedness is a crucial step <u>towards</u> Knowledge, but it still is a part of the illusion, even if the illusion starts to be "The Happy World".

> "Right-mindedness is not to be confused with the knowing mind, because it is applicable only to right perception.
> You can be right-minded or wrong-minded, and even this is subject to degrees, clearly demonstrating that knowledge is not involved. The term "right-mindedness" is properly used as the correction for "wrong-mindedness," and applies to

> the state of mind that induces accurate perception. It is miracle-minded because it heals misperception, and this is indeed a miracle in view of how you perceive yourself."
> (T-3.IV.4)

Or, as Clarification of Terms explains (C-1.5):

> "The mind can be right or wrong, depending on the voice to which it listens. Right-mindedness listens to the Holy Spirit, forgives the world, and through Christ's vision sees the real world in its place. This is the final vision, the last perception, the condition in which God takes the final step Himself. Here time and illusions end together."

So, remember — there are no "good" people and "bad" people, they are <u>all</u> Brothers and Sisters, being <u>either</u> Right-minded <u>or</u> Wrong-minded. Or sometimes one, at other times, the other...

And, even if emotions might be experienced as very varied, as described eloquently as in John's table Levels of Emotions, there are really only two basic emotions behind them all — fear and love. And these are mutually excluding, and one of them can dispel the other, either way...

For us reading ACIM a lot, discussing it, working with it, meditating on it, we may forget the "basics", and it may in this context be useful to recapitulate the very first sentences:

> "Nothing real can be threatened.
>
> Nothing unreal exists.
>
> Herein lies the peace of God."

Until next time, with love

Lena Adamson

~.~.~.~. * .~.~.~.~

Stairway   Lars Gimstedt

October 15, 2348. NSA Report.

****

NSA Report 2346-1001-4919
TOP SECRET. CLF code 0.
Department for The Transhuman Threat.
October 15 2348.
Unmonitored disappearances.
Case study TTT-JZ-1.

****

Still no traces of JZ, almost half a year after his disappearance March 21.

The Four Unions Treaty has resulted in the governing global policy The Trust Document, establishing Mutual Trust as the core value. NSA_TTT is presently evaluating and analyzing the security effects of this policy change.

It has become very difficult to maintain TSS integrity, especially after UN support has suddenly decreased, as they have officially announced doubts about surveillance, claiming that it engenders fear and suspicion, instead of making people feel secure.

Due to the return of confused and conflicting management from the UN and from NSA, all NSA-TTT personnel have again been moved back to the secret locations outside the US.

As we are unable to assess internal integrity of the NSA-TTT organization, our sub-department has decided to isolate ourselves from the rest of NSA-TTT, and we have got information that others sub-departments have done the same.

These reports therefore from now on reflect only the activities from NSA-TTT-5. The staff number is now 950, but unfortunately decreasing with several defecting agents each month, and no means for external re-staffing.

****

End of NSA Report 2346-1001-4919
TOP SECRET. CLF code 0.
October 15 2348.

****

Stairway   Lars Gimstedt

October 30, 2348.
Stairway New Zealand News.

Dear Sisters and Brothers

Still no news about John. We will keep you posted.

Mankind has taken another giant step towards The Happy Dream, a peaceful world, with the Four Unions' new agreement, The Trust Document. At the Center, we will celebrate this with a special Moon Imagine Peace Tower meditation now on **Friday December 3 at 8:30 PM.**

~.~. * .~.~

My input about The Last days, The Tribulation, The Second Coming in the newsletter June 30 have led to many comments via com and in person from members. Many have asked why I have written about these ancient Bible notions, as all ACIM students know well how these things are interpreted completely different in ACIM.

The positive world events and the different ways the Stairway movement has been involved in these have caused counter-reactions from many fundamentalist groups, accusing us to go "the devil's errands". So the reason I write about the Biblical ideas is to clarify and to remind you about how they can be interpreted in ways that harmonize with ACIM.

It is also to remind you of the importance of not responding to judgment from others with counter-judgment. When you become attacked, when criticized, when judged by others, find your Inner Peace first, remind yourself of all the lessons on how to perceive with Love, and _then_ respond.

> Lesson 21: I am determined to see things differently.
>
> Lesson 34: I could see peace instead of this.
>
> Lesson 46: God is the Love in which I forgive.
>
> Lesson 48: There is nothing to fear.

People and right-wing media have tried to scare us with The Last Judgment, and it might be helpful to remind yourself about ACIM's re-definition of this term, as when it answers the question "Is each one to be judged at the end?"

> "Indeed, yes! No one can escape God's Final Judgment. Who could flee forever from the truth? But the Final Judgment will not come until it is no longer associated with fear.
>
> One day each one will welcome it, and on that very day it will be given him. He will hear his sinlessness proclaimed around and around the world, setting it free as God's Final Judgment on him is received.
>
> This is the Judgment in which salvation lies. This is the Judgment that will set him free. This is the Judgment in which all things are freed with him. Time pauses as eternity comes near, and silence lies across the world that everyone may hear this Judgment of the Son of God:

Holy are you, eternal, free and whole, at peace forever in the Heart of God.

Where is the world, and where is sorrow now?

Is this your judgment on yourself, teacher of God? Do you believe that this is wholly true? No; not yet, not yet. But this is still your goal; why you are here. It is your function to prepare yourself to hear this Judgment and to recognize that it is true."
(Manual, M-15.1)

~.~. * .~.~

Until next time, with love

Lena Adamson

~.~.~.~. * .~.~.~.~

Stairway   Lars Gimstedt

December 25, 2348.
BLOG ENTRY: Bestowing Bliss – Oneness.

Step	Stage	Aspect
10.	Bestowing Bliss.	Oneness.
9.	The Origin.	The Vision.
8.	Man Forgotten.	The Mission.
7.	Bull Forgotten.	Self-image.
6.	Returning Home.	Values.
5.	Gentling the Bull.	Beliefs.
4.	Catching the Bull.	Reality.
3.	Finding the Bull.	Skill.
2.	Finding Traces.	Action.
1.	Seeks.	Context.

Stairway

Lars Gimstedt

Beloved Brothers, beloved Sisters.

This will be the last blog entry you will receive from me, because after we have celebrated Christmas and New Year's Eve together at the Reykjavik Center, and we have bid farewell to all our friends here, four of us here at the Center will depart by time-jump January 1 next year. We are not going Home yet, but into the future.

Before you get alarmed, please read this blog entry carefully. I am confident that after you have read it, and taken in what I am telling you, you will feel the same peace and anticipation as I do!

I have been away the larger part of this year, but I think many of you have drawn the conclusion from Petur Bjarnason's hints, that I would come back today, to celebrate Christmas together with you all. I have this time not been anywhere, as I came here with time jump two weeks after making my latest blog entry in March 21.

This is the first example of what I from now on will continue to do: by economizing what may remain of my physical existence by being here short periods only, with longer periods of time in between, I can meet my still insatiable need to satisfy my curiosity...

But to be honest, the plan for this came to me in a third encounter with the Fisherman one week after having written my last blog entry, where He asked me to fulfil my Mission as Senior Adviser at a number of different time periods in the future.

This plan makes me of course feel a bit nervous, with all the unpredictability it involves, but I am sure He knows what He is doing… But at the same time it feels good that I may be of more help by "spreading out" my physical existence over a larger period of time.

Next jump will bring us to a time exactly fifty years in the future, returning here on Videy, so many of you I will probably meet again. Jumps after this might be longer, I will decide each time depending on how the situation develops (or I will get new orders…). As I will be accompanied in the coming jump by three persons close to me, I will probably not have the same feeling of loss that I experienced after my three hundred year jump.

As we cannot jump backwards in time (thank God for that…) this blog entry is also, as I said, my farewell to many of you out in the world. I feel blessed to have gotten the opportunity to participate in everything wonderful that has taken place the last two years, and I feel thankful for all the Holy Encounters I have had, with so many of you.

As there is only a week left before our departure, I might not be able to answer all com messages I get, but I will do my best. The messages I do not answer myself, will be handled by Petur Bjarnason, our Information Manager.

***

But for now, I am fulfilling the last parts of my Mission, together with many others of you:

> *Lesson 353. My eyes, my tongue, my hands, my feet today Have but one purpose; to be given Christ to use to bless the world with miracles.*

> *Lesson 360. Peace be to me, the holy Son of God. Peace to my brother, who is one with me. Let all the world be blessed with peace through us.*

With the new global policy, The Trust Document, signed by The Four Unions and by the UN, world peace will now soon be in place.

Even if there still is unrest in many places, more and more of us are starting to attain True Perception, by which we cannot yet see and experience Truth, but which *points* at Truth. This gives hope, and hope leads to Inner Peace.

***

I have been back for two weeks only, but I have already got many questions about what will happen now. Many of these questions have been about the issue of The Second Coming of Christ.

Stairway

I can assure you, that the Second Coming is not about a person. It stands for a radical transformation of all our minds. It has not happened yet, but what has happened the last months gives hope!

ACIM describes The Second Coming like this, just before Lesson 300:

> *The Second Coming is the one event in time which time itself can not affect. For every one who ever came to die, or yet will come or who is present now, is equally released from what he made. In this equality is Christ restored as one Identity, in which the Sons of God acknowledge that they all are one.*
>
> *And God the Father smiles upon His Son, His one creation and His only joy.*
>
> *Pray that the Second Coming will be soon, but do not rest with that. It needs your eyes and ears and hands and feet. It needs your voice. And most of all it needs your willingness.*
>
> *Let us rejoice that we can do God's Will, and join together in its holy light. Behold, the Son of God is one in us, and we can reach our Father's Love through Him.*

Different time, same place

In this blog I will, as in the ones before, continue to tell you about my personal path to awakening. Today

Stairway Lars Gimstedt

I will describe the time from when I arrived here after my three hundred year jump until today, a little more than two years.

This will conclude my story, for many of you. For those of you that might decide to follow me into the future, keep following this blog, as I intend to keep it active as long as possible, by updating it during my visits on Earth.

As I told you in my last blog entry, I came out of transit at noon September 19 2346, and I stood on the shore of Videy, at the northwest point of the island. I walked the two kilometers to the Center, which I could soon observe had expanded tremendously during the 300 years that now had passed. Apart from the old central building and the four wings, I saw that many new house complexes had been built higher up the hill, towards the Imagine Peace Tower, which I could see still was in place.

I felt quite nervous – I had no idea what would meet me. The Center might, for all I knew, have become the Iceland headquarters for NSA...

But, when I arrived, and entered the central lobby, some remote sensor had obviously been picking up my arrival, and I was met by a large group of people with Stairway logos on their clothes. One of them stepped forward, and greeted me by my name, which surprised me, until I happened to look behind the group: on the front wall on the opposite wall of the entrance, there was a large portrait of me, lit from the inside.

Stairway   Lars Gimstedt

The woman who greeted me presented herself as the manager of the Center; it was Gudrid Thorbjarnardóttir. She presented me to the Information Manager, Petur Bjarnason. These two were the ones that the coming weeks helped me to settle in and to adjust to the new time era.

They now presented me to each one of the other staff members. Many of them seemed first very shy, and it felt as I was being treated as if I was some kind of god descended from the heavens to Earth. But after a while everybody relaxed, me included, and being there almost felt as before, only with new people.

Many of them told me that my awaited return had become somewhat of a myth, and how there had been a constant speculation going on about when I would return. The expressed their gratitude to me over the fact that I had chosen *them*, but I tried to convince them that *I* had not chosen the time, or chosen them, but that Jesus probably had, by reasons hidden from me.

To my great surprise and satisfaction, my and Hi'ilani's old apartment had been preserved as a museum, and I could move in with no special arrangements other than learning how to use the new dining room, which had been equipped with a food synthesizer instead of the old kitchen corner, and getting used to the levitation bed (which made wonders to my old creaky joints).

Already the day after, we were contacted by NSA people that wanted to come to the Center and interrogate me (the TSS had of course detected my arrival). They landed soon after their com call just outside the entrance with a flying vehicle with lev-drive that to me, being "a stone-age man" in this context, seemed as pure magic. We had a good meeting, where I tried to explain the principles of space-time-jumps to them, and they dutifully made notes in their coms, but my feeling was that they did not believe me at all. Rather, I felt, they suspected me to trying to divert them from "the truth" by what they regarded as fairy tales...

The first weeks were extremely busy. Petur was in charge of a tight plan, which included short daily meetings with visitors, two hours per day where Petur briefed me in the history of Earth from 2046 up to present time, including the development of Stairway, which had grown tremendously.

I was pleased to hear that they had "broken the code" of space jump travel, attaining the intuitive knowledge and learnt the meditation discipline needed, even if it had taken them a good one hundred years, and there were a few at the Center as well as other Stairway centers that had developed the ability to transit location-wise, but not yet time-wise. They said they were looking forward to me leading them in practicing, so that they could learn how to jump in time as well as in space. (A number of them have now learned this, as you maybe knew before, and which I told you about in the beginning of this blog entry.)

Stairway Lars Gimstedt

The last stop

In the time period following the first two "adjustment weeks", I spent a lot of time transiting to the different Stairway Centers, the number of which amazed me, to have meetings with many of the new local managers.

After each of these trips, I had to go through a new interrogation by NSA agents. They were obviously very disturbed by how transiting affected their surveillance equipment. They have some kind of theory about brain fields called BQRF, which they obviously wanted me to confirm. So when I tried to explain to them that the brain is no transmitter of anything, it is more like a com receiver, and on top of that in itself the result of our mental projections, one of them even lost his temper for a while.

What had made things worse for them was all the Stairway members with transit capability, and what the agents called TSS disconnects obviously happened all the time now, which I gathered from them was causing severe problems in the system.

After an initially busy time period, I also took time to be by myself, which took some adjusting – the grief of having lost my life companion for fifty years, Hi'ilani, became very strong when I finally had time to myself. I was relieved to learn that the rest of her life until 2053, when she passed away peacefully, had been a time of harmony and spiritual growth. All the holos of her and of my family that the Center had stored in their internal com net, helped me to work through my grief, and after a while it abated to a tender sadness and also to deep gratefulness.

After a while, I got more used to being alone, and could even appreciate the opportunity to expand my meditation times to be four hours a day.

As I was aware of the fact that The Holy Spirit, talking through the Fisherman in my dreams, had asked me to come here with a purpose, I meditated a lot on this, concentrating on the last one of the images in The Bull and His Herdsman – "Entering The Market Place with Bliss-bestowing Hands" :

With the role I wanted to have, Senior Adviser, I had a hard time recognizing myself in the text beneath the image:

> *The brush-wood gate is firmly shut and neither sage nor Buddha can see him. He has deeply buried his light and permits himself to differ from the well-established ways of the old masters.*

> *Carrying a gourd, he enters the market; twirling his staff, he returns home. He frequents wine-shops and fish-stalls to make the drunkards open their eyes and awaken to themselves.*

But it felt like the text told me: let go of all your preconceived ideas of what it is to be an ascended master – be yourself. Or rather, Be your Self. And this thought made me relax: if I just remained in my knowledge of who I was, and listened inwards, I would know what to do.

ACIM says that one of the important traits of a God's Teacher is honesty:

> *Honesty does not apply only to what you say. The term actually means consistency.*
>
> *There is nothing you say that contradicts what you think or do; no thought opposes any other thought; no act belies your word; and no word lacks agreement with another.*
>
> *Such are the truly honest. At no level are they in conflict with themselves. Therefore it is impossible for them to be in conflict with anyone or anything.*
>
> *(M-4.II.1)*

The second part of the "Bull" text seemed to tell me: by all means keep talking with the ones who want to listen, the ones that trust you. But, also start to talk with those who do *not* want to listen, and who might *not* trust you.

Stairway   Lars Gimstedt

Trust miracles to happen, even if they happen through your subconscious mind, and if you do not see any results:

> *Miracles are expressions of love,*
> *but they may not always have observable effects.*
>
> *(Miracle Principle 35, T-1.I.)*

Or, as the first poem under the Bull image describes:

> *Bare-chested and bare-footed*
> *he enters the market,*
>
> *Face streaked with dust*
> *and head covered with ashes,*
>
> *But a mighty laugh spreads*
> *from cheek to cheek.*
>
> *Without troubling himself to work miracles,*
> *suddenly dead trees break into bloom.*

Entering The Market Place with Bliss-bestowing Hands.

I meditated on the third poem for a long period of time:

> *From out of his sleeve the iron jumps*
> *right into the face.*
>
> *Genially and full of laughter,*
>
> *He may talk Mongolian, or speak in Chinese.*

Stairway — Lars Gimstedt

> *Wide open the palace gates to him who,*
> *meeting himself, yet remains unknown to himself.*

It seemed to say: As long as I am honest, as long I am my Self, and as long I let what I say and do be inspired by The Holy Spirit, and I keep forgetting myself, "the palace gates will open".

As a result of these thoughts, *I* started to ask for meetings with leaders in the world, instead of only meeting with those that had asked for meetings with me.

And I found that the less I explained why I wanted to talk to them, and the less I tried to explain what I wanted to talk about, the more "palace doors" opened.

I could even arrive in a country somewhere un-announced, and ask to have a meeting with some political leader, an industry leader, or a religious leader, and immediately get access.

Often these kind of meetings were the most fruitful, where people had not prepared agendas and visiting programs. I had many fine meetings where we could just sit at talk on a personal level, getting to know each other, exchanging ideas and thoughts. These informal meetings were also very often followed up, where the person I had asked to meet wanted to meet again, and in these cases they often took the time to travel to Iceland, where the surrounding could be more informal and relaxed than in their "palaces" –

government offices, industry headquarters, religious centers.

And for me, the expression *"From out of his sleeve the iron jumps right into the face"* meant presenting an idea the person I talked with had not thought about before, an idea that could take root, sometimes at once, sometimes a long time after. I liked that the expression, that by itself felt somewhat offensive to me, is followed by *"Genially and full of laughter"*, as this matched well the self-image I wanted to have.

New core values

As you all have been able to observe, and to participate in, the gradual awakening of mankind has during this last year come into a phase of a very rapid awakening, involving more and more people.

Many of the awakening ones have been in leadership positions, and have together with each other, across national and cultural borders, established new core values for mankind, values as Openness, Honesty and Trust.

The collective transiting Home by the Lhasa Center in June earlier this year scared many first, but over the time that has passed since it has been a source of curiosity, awe and inspiration.

For myself, the returning home of the Dalai Lhama and others there caused me grief, as he and many there had become close friends. But all I feel today is awe, hope and "Divine Home-sickness".

Stairway — Lars Gimstedt

During this year, we have all become witnesses to, or victims of, a lot of violence and civil unrest, even short wars. I see this happening as the last "convulsions" of the collective ego, trying to with all it's might to regain its power over our collective mind. But, I assure you: it is now finally losing this war. Not because we are fighting back, but because untruth can never in the end "win" over Truth. Fear, in the face of unconditional Love, can only abate, opening up for relief and peace. Light always dispels darkness, darkness can never by itself dispel light.

Oneness

I have come to the end of my story of my personal awakening.

I have been privileged to participate in the start of a collective awakening of mankind, for which I am deeply grateful.

I, and many with me, have come to the last step of "The Stairway to Heaven".

As you may remember, in my blog entries from May 18 and July 20 2347 and March 21 this year, I presented a table "Levels of Emotions":

Stairway — Lars Gimstedt

Level	Emotion	Thought proc.	Self-image	Image of God
ILLUMINATION	(Indescribable)	**Presence**	I Am	I Am
PEACE	Bliss	Enlightenment	I am perfect	In everything
HAPPINESS	Joy	Transformation	I am whole	Embracing
LOVE	Love	Revelation	I am kind	Loving
REASON	Empathy	Abstraction	I am needed	Wise
ACCEPTANCE	Forgiveness	Transcendence	I am human	Compassionate
WILL	Optimism	Creation	I want	Inspiring
NEUTRALITY	Trust	Tolerance	I am OK	Creative
COURAGE	Firmness	Observance	I am growing	Allowing

I myself have not yet reached the highest level in this table, but I feel that I have not far to go. In short ecstatic glimpses during my meditations, or when I get an intense sense of one-ness with a person I meet, I sometimes experience an "indescribable" emotion, that affects me stronger than empathy, love, joy, even bliss.

In these "Holy Instants" I experience myself as the simplest self-images of all, just "I am", and in this experiencing a complete oneness with God, who describes Himself equally simple – "I Am".

ACIM describes The Holy Instant like this:

> *You will recognize it with perfect certainty. No gift of God is recognized in any other way.*
>
> *You can practice the mechanics of the holy instant, and will learn much from doing so.*
>
> *Yet its shining and glittering brilliance, which will literally blind you to this world by its own vision, you cannot supply.*

> *And here it is, all in this instant, complete, accomplished and given wholly.*

(T-15.II.5)

The Happy Dream

With this, this blog entry has come to its end. I will return with more, in the future. My age, even with the fine treatment I get from the doctors here at the Center, makes part of me wanting to stay, to just dwell here in peace, but both my curiosity and the Fisherman are both pushing me ahead...

I hope I will be able to live in my physical reality a long while more, and I feel that my curiosity of what will emerge will boost my health. My curiosity and my longing to see, experience and participate in what ACIM calls "The Happy Dream", which will be mankind's last step before we all return Home.

And to experience how this is the result of something that at first maybe was limited to "a little willingness" in many, and that after a while also was the result also of dedication, persistence, practice and vigilance in more and more of us.

Vigilance to let The Holy Spirit, Christ and God come into our minds, for Them to dispel the "bad dream". ACIM describes the "Happy Dream" like this:

> *The blood of hatred fades to let the grass grow green again, and let the flowers be all white and sparkling in the summer sun.*

Stairway
Lars Gimstedt

> *What was a place of death has now become a living temple in a world of light. Because of Them.*
>
> *It is Their Presence which has lifted holiness again to take its ancient place upon an ancient throne.*
>
> *Because of Them have miracles sprung up as grass and flowers on the barren ground that hate had scorched and rendered desolate. What hate has wrought have They undone.*
>
> *And now you stand on ground so holy Heaven leans to join with it, and make it like itself. The shadow of an ancient hate has gone, and all the blight and withering have passed forever from the land where They have come.*
>
> *(T-26.IX.3.)*

***

With this, I say Amen.

Remember to participate in the next Moon Imagine Peace Tower meditation on Monday January 3 next year, at times during the day that will be announced by your local center.

I hope what the Iceland Stairway Center has arranged together with the UN, World Meditation on Peace, will be a success. Even if I will not be here in person, I have prepared a surprise for this event.

Stairway   Lars Gimstedt

So, I say farewell for now. See you all back Home!

John Zacharias

Stairway   Lars Gimstedt

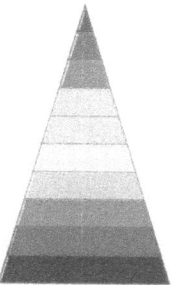

December 30, 2348.
Stairway New Zealand News.

Dearest Sisters and Brothers

All of you have surely read John's blog entry on Christmas Day, so you of course know: John is leaving us the day after tomorrow. He has been with us from September 19 2046, a little more than two years.

During this time, more wonderful things have happened here on Earth, than most of us could ever have dreamed of, even in our wildest dreams. The ironic thing is that we <u>could</u> have done it, as this <u>is</u> a dream. But, as a part of a collective mind, from the level of <u>my</u> individual mind, <u>I</u> could not have dreamt of this outcome.

I have taken the freedom to send John a farewell message from us all here on New Zealand. In this message I have expressed our gratitude to him and to

Stairway   Lars Gimstedt

Jesus, for having given us the gift of The Happy Dream that now seems to emerge. I have not received any response from him yet, and we might not get one — his schedule must be pretty tight just now... But if and when I get one, I will distribute it in a newsletter at once.

I am really looking forward to his return fifty years from now. All of us relatively young will probably still be here when this happens, and many of you that have reached older ages might be here as well, having jumped themselves in time.

In order to keep John alive in our memories, we have put up a newly taken photo of him, to the right of the old one, in our front lobby.

~.~. * .~.~

Even if you of course know it via all the media ads, I want to remind you of the meditation now on **Monday January 3 2349 at 6:00 to 9:00 PM, inside the Mount Eden crater here in Auckland.**

Here the New Zealand government has arranged, together with the Reykjavik Stairway Center, our local broadcast of the World Peace Meditation. It will be led by **John Zacharias** (!) via VR holographic recording. This event is part of a world-wide event that Stairway and the UN have arranged together.

The meditation gathering will be opened by our friend Petur Bjarnason. The VR recording of John was made on Christmas Eve, when he led his staff at the Reykjavik Center through the meditation.

In addition to the seating arrangements inside the crater, a number of other sites have been prepared all over New Zealand, where one can participate in the meditation via large screen. (Look at your local town's web site for info.)

I, for one, am really looking forward to this truly **World Event**: this meditation will be transmitted to all Asian countries as well. John's meditation will be sent out another three more times in intervals of six hours. The four meditations will be transmitted to all countries of the world at different times, depending on which time zone they are in.

At Mount Eden, at the end if the meditation which will be three hours long, we will be able to see the Moon Imagine Peace Tower. This will be the case for all other

Stairway   Lars Gimstedt

Stairway Centers as well, but at different times during the World Peace Meditation.

~.~. * .~.~

Except for this piece of information, I have felt reluctant to write anything more in this newsletter, as I feel that John's latest blog entry speaks for itself. If you haven't read it yet, do.

Or, it is more than reluctance – I really feel overwhelmed by awe and gratitude for everything that is unfolding on Earth just now, so

I hope I will see you all on Mount Eden!

Lena Adamson

~.~.~.~. * .~.~.~.~

Stairway Lars Gimstedt

January 9, 2349. NSA Report.

****

NSA Report 2346-1001-5080
TOP SECRET. CLF code 0.
Department for The Transhuman Threat.
January 9 2349. TERMINATION REPORT
Unmonitored disappearances.
Case study TTT-JZ-1.

****

To whom it may concern:

This may be the last report issued by NSA-TTT-5. We only have twenty agents left, our resources for continuing are soon depleted, as the NSA has ceased to exist except as a juridical entity.

We do not know to whom to send this report, so it will just be filed in the part of the NSA net still working, for future follow-up of the activities of this department.

During last week, the TSS crashed completely, and when information about this leaked to the public, massive destruction activities took place. In these, that had the character of folk feasts with bonfires and celebrating, all TSS probes were located, destroyed and put on the bonfires.

Due to the TSS crash, and due to no liaison with any other NSA offices, or any other authority offices for that matter, the only method for gathering information from now on is by infiltration with our few remaining agents. Our ability to influence or control has been reduced to nil.

As JZ evidently has returned, we conclude that the above described events have been initiated by him or by others in Stairway, but due to complete of lack of other information other than what is available to the public via the net, we do not know this for sure. JZ's blog entry Dec 25 gives no hints about this, except for the fact that he seems to support the civil unrest.

According to JZ's blog he disappeared again January 1, but due to lack of both TSS probes and on-site agents we have not been able to verify this. This time he has disclosed the date for his return to January 1 2999. But, as many now seem to have the same capabilities that JZ acquired three hundred years ago, JZ as a person does not require the same focus from NSA-TTT as before. Rather, we have to concentrate on analyzing how a rapidly increasing number of Transhumans will affect life on Earth.

From media, we have gathered that almost all of the governments in the world have asked to become involved in a world-wide agreement equal to The Trust Document established October last year, and that they have asked the Stairway Movement to provide experts for the new offices planned to be put in place next year.

These new government offices will take on the task of reforming all legislature to conform to the Trust Document. In the instructions, there seems to be a definite diversion from the former security principles of the UN.

We therefore reluctantly feel forced to report that we foresee a complete termination of NSA and all organizations connected to NSA.

****

End of NSA Report 2346-1001-5080
TOP SECRET. CLF code 0.
January 9 2349. TERMINATION REPORT

****

Appendix A: Key events

2021	Stairway to Heaven is published.
2024	JZ visits the 14:th Dalai Lhama.
2030	Stairway HQ moves to Iceland.
2033	Second Imagine Peace Tower, Lhasa
2039	Yoko Ono dies.
2040	JZ's first space-time jump.
2043	First pure climate-related wars.
2046	JZ disappears.
Sept 19 2346	JZ reappears.
July 2347	First killing of Stairway member in Madurai, India. First documented resurrection.
Sept	JZ visits the Pope. Peace Treaty China-India. 18:th Dalai Lhama moves to Lhasa, the Lhasa Stairway Center relocates to the palace.
Nov	JZ makes first outer space jump, to the inauguration of Imagine Peace Tower on the Moon Base.
Dec 25	Stairway communicates on global media for first time.

Feb 2348   Tibet free again, after 400 years.

June   First collective disappearance, whole Stairway Center Lhasa.

Oct   The Trust Document. NSA-TTT crumbles.

Dec   World Peace Project initiated.
           NSA closed down.

www.ingramcontent.com/pod-product-compliance
Lightning Source LLC
Chambersburg PA
CBHW071148160426
43196CB00011B/2047